TO PLAY ALONG
THE PATH

*The Multifarious Ps of Existential
Philosophy & Practice*

RICHARD V. CAMPAGNA

1st WORLD
PUBLISHING

TO PLAY ALONG THE PATH

RICHARD V. CAMPAGNA

© Richard V. Campagna 2008

Published by 1stWorld Publishing
1100 North 4th St. Fairfield, Iowa 52556
tel: 641-209-5000 • fax: 641-209-3001
web: www.1stworldpublishing.com

First Edition

LCCN: 2008924412
SoftCover ISBN: 978-1-4218-9856-8
HardCover ISBN: 978-1-4218-9855-1
eBook ISBN: 978-1-4218-9857-5

This material has been written and published solely for educational purposes. The author and the publisher shall have neither liability or responsibility to any person or entity with respect to any loss, damage or injury caused or alleged to be caused directly or indirectly by the information contained in this book.

The characters and events described in this text are intended to entertain and teach rather than present an exact factual history of real people or events.

"We should act as if our lives will last forever, as if our energies were limitless, as if we could do anything and everything we choose, as if we had no personal constraints.

Knowing we are doomed to fail in this quest, but developing faith in ourselves, through ongoing self-reflection, loving conversations with others and with a higher force, this is the essence of optimistic, spiritual existentialism, with a libertarian twist."

Table of Contents

Foreword. 9
by Richard Campagna

I. Not All Who Wander Are Lost!. 17
by Sarah M. Haaf

II. The Moral Necessity of Personal Freedom 25
by Peter Catsimpiris

III. Existential Psychology. 43
by LeAnn Gentry

IV. Existentialism & Education 57
by Mary T. Haaf and Austin C. Wedemeyer

V. Programmed Performance Enhancing Drug
Use In Sport: Cheating The Spontaneous Spirit
of Competition 61
by Dr. Gary Gaffney

VI. Physical Perfections or Physique Perversions?
Appearance Enhancing Drugs, Procedures And
The Natural Life. 71
by Dr. Gary Gaffney

VII. Existentialism & Judicial Realism 81
by Richard Campagna

VIII. Walter Jay Greenberg—Existentialist Par Excellence . 87
by Walter Jay Greenberg

IX. Medical Existentialism. 109
   by Dr. Laurie Margolies

X. Simply And Profoundly Christy 115
   by Christy Ann Welty

XI. The Endless Road—Existentialism &
   Political Freedom 133
   by Ed Noyes, Esq.

XII. Dos & Don'ts 141
   by Richard Campagna

Afterword—The Saga of Lena Hill 149
   by Richard Campagna

About the Author 151

Foreword

by Richard Campagna

This is a particularly challenging and inspiring time for myself and my family and close knit community of friends and colleagues as we traverse together an optimistic, existential, spiritual path of life. I will endeavor to explain why I assert the foregoing in these prefatory remarks to this work, "TO PLAY ALONG THE PATH."

I was the first of four (4) children of a mixed marriage (religiously and culturally speaking, not racially), born in Brooklyn, New York on May 5, 1952. My mother was deemed to be (and really was, by all known accounts), "a nice Jewish girl from Brooklyn." My father was a soft-spoken Italo-American intellectual from the Bronx, whose own father was once a chef in the Italian Navy. The above-described potpourri of religious beliefs, cultural proclivities and personality styles most definitely made me the man I am today—a compassionate, easy-going, existential, spiritual, intellectually honest, hard working libertarian who doesn't have much time for excessive manifestations of materialism, philosophical bullshit nor political correctness, hypocrisy and corruption. (Does this bring to mind any current political leaders?)

My early years in Brooklyn took place during the era which one best selling author characterized as "When Brooklyn Was The World." Life was anything but "existentially confusing." I attended P.S. 152, Andrés Hudde (a French pirate) Junior High School and Midwood High School (alma mater of Woody Allen and other luminaries) amidst a highly competitive bunch of mostly Jewish classmates, whose passion in life, engendered by their Depression Era parents, was to "get into an Ivy League School or their lives would be ruined." Most of my fellow students, including myself, dutifully complied with our parents' most fervent desires and incorporated them as our own.

These were very happy years for me, despite the fact that I "skipped" two and a half grades of school, thereby relegating me to being every pretty girl's best friend or younger brother figure. The dearth of romantic love and athletic dominance during my adolescence would be made up for many times over during my subsequent years as an international corporate attorney and businessman, to be discussed hereinafter.

I attended Brown University in Providence, R.I., commencing when I was barely 16 years of age and to this day I credit Brown and my first large corporate employer, Schlumberger Ltd., with engendering in me an optimistic, existential, spiritual and libertarian approach to love and life, as well as an indefatigable self-confidence.

"Cut the bullshit" has been my battle cry for the past 40+ years and will continue to be so until my dying days. I developed this motto while observing the political affiliations of both of my parents, my mother having been a long time Democratic Party Leader in Brooklyn, my father a long time "Rockefeller Republican" appointee, in the role of State Tax Commissioner. Ultimately, my parents' disappointment with the ideologies, procedures and personalities of their respective political parties, particularly my mother, probably resulted in my drifting towards Libertarianism at the beginning of the new millennium.

As if these political disappointments weren't enough heartache for my well-intentioned parents, my beloved sister Andrea was tragically killed in an automobile accident in 1972, at the tender age of 17, which event, although not properly grieved due to the prevailing cultural mores of the times, had perhaps the most profound effect on my life as well as the lives of the rest of my family. At that time, drunk drivers who often caused tremendous pain and suffering to their victims and their families, were not treated as the criminals they truly were.

Soon after my sister's death, I attended St. John's University Law School and simultaneously completed a Masters Degree in Ibero-American Studies at New York University. Upon my simultaneous graduations from these fine educational institutions, I headed off to Caracas Venezuela in late 1975, to work as an international lawyer, a college instructor (teaching a course in Existential Literature), administrator, writer and diplomat. Mixing and matching jobs, careers, girlfriends and the like, not accepting pre-packaged life styles and being intellectually honest with myself and others, continue to this day to be my guiding trademarks. During this period of my life, I connected with my wonderful wife of 33 years, Odalys Perez-Medina and together we visited over 190 countries, some of which no longer exist, plus all 50 states and all of our dependencies, on numerous occasions.

During the late 1970's and early 1980's we lived and worked in Caracas, Rio, Bogotá, Paris, London and the San Francisco Bay area, having the times of our lives. For much of that time, I particularly lived like an international jet-setter and self-styled playboy, with all that such life-styles entail. I will always be grateful to Odalys for understanding my promiscuity during that period of my life, inasmuch as I believed I was making up for lost time in high school when sex and romance were hard to come by for me, because of my chronological age. I never ceased to love my wife, even though my outward behavior might have suggested otherwise at times.

In 1982, in odd and abrupt fashion and for reasons which many people still do not understand, I voluntarily gave up all of the corporate glitz and we returned to New York City, Brooklyn Heights to be exact, to spend time with my parents who were to meet their untimely demises (despite a lifetime of good health and happiness) due to the traumatic after shocks of losing their wonderful daughter, my wonderful sister, at the hands of the previously mentioned drunk driver.

My wife, our first and only son Robert and I lived in Brooklyn Heights for almost nine years where I valiantly (my choice of word) endeavored to develop multiple enterprises and professional practices, in true "existential, free-wheeling" fashion. A law practice, consulting firm, boutique travel agency (as it is described in Wikipedia) specializing in travel to Cuba for American journalists as well as public speaking engagements, were all within my "grab-bag" of activities. But while I was good at all of the foregoing, I couldn't put these diverse activities together in a financially viable fashion, within the difficult constraints of the "newly developing global economy" and the dizzying advances of "information technology" which were rapidly passing me by.

Searching for something more meaningful for myself, my family and for society at large, during our unique "trip" through life…and further fed up with the Democratic Party Machine, which had control of New York City and most of New York State, we decided to pack it all in and leave the city where my family had long and deep roots (considering we were a family of immigrants) and a high psychological comfort level. Incidentally, at the time, David Dinkins was serving as the first African-American mayor of NYC and Mario M. Cuomo (my former eloquent law professor and family friend) was Governor. Both were doing a rather poor job in my view, in terms of their governance of The Big Apple and The Empire State, respectively.

The City was in shambles...with urine and vomit stinking up our beloved Grand Central Station. Garbage was slow to be collected and squeegee men and other diverse criminals were terrorizing our streets and public places. The murder rate was soaring...and crack addicts were roaming the streets, looking to score at all costs...including taking the lives of thousands of innocent New Yorkers.

I packed up my car one fateful Saturday morning and loaded my recently acquired Masters Degree from Columbia University Teachers College in Psychological Counseling (my wife was pursuing one in Latin American literature at the same institution) and we headed overland to Iowa, The Hawkeye State, to pursue Doctorates in Counseling Psychology and Spanish/Portuguese Linguistics/Literature, respectively. We were seeking a "heartland" experience for our son, the pride and joy of our lives; such an experience was something that neither my wife nor myself had ever really had. We wanted a nice, modern house with a large backyard, not a million dollar squished up Brownstone with mold and crab grass growing around every corner....and we wanted to be able to park our cars effortlessly, attend high school football games and cheer on our son and his peers and then spend long summer weekends at Wisconsin Dells. We accomplished all of the foregoing and much, much more than that during our 17+ years in Iowa, which still endure at the time of publication of this book.

While attempting to acculturate to our new Midwestern neighbors, mixing and meshing once again with diverse groups in Iowa, groups with whom we hadn't had much contact in New York City (farmers, Bohemians, homeless men and women, German American Catholics, Big Ten College students, migrant farm workers from Mexico, Irish blue collar workers), I continued to practice, refine, develop and preach my long-time philosophy of "optimistic, spiritual, existentialism," leaving traditional politics in the distant past.

That is, until 2001, when a charismatic gentleman from Hammond, Indiana, by way of Fairfield Iowa, named Clyde Cleveland (a distant relative of our one-time president Grover), spoke at the Iowa City Public Library, together with Ed Noyes, a contributor to this book. Clyde announced that he was throwing his hat in the ring for Governor of Iowa, declaring as a Libertarian, one year in advance of the November 2002 elections. Cleveland was and still is an eloquent speaker and the fact that he was declaring his candidacy one year in advance of the election, on behalf of a small third party, seemed like a very gutsy, optimistic, existential thing to do!

Both my wife and myself had some contact with Libertarian political ideology during our undergraduate college years and we attended a couple of Libertarian events in Brooklyn many years ago, but quite frankly, hadn't done much more. As previously indicated, I had washed my hands of the whole tawdry mess of politics since we left NYC in 1991.

But Cleveland's methodical, historical explanation of "bottom-up government" and his motivational style of public address got me going in a way that I hadn't experienced for quite a while. Within weeks, I was to become his running mate for Lt. Governor of Iowa and within a couple of years, I would be named the Libertarian Party's nominee for Vice President of The United States, attempting to integrate "personal and professional existential philosophy" with Libertarian political ideology. I hope to expand a bit upon the trials and tribulations of both of these campaigns and their aftermath in the pages that follow and in my next book, as we lead up to the tumultuous and earth shattering Presidential elections of 2008.

It is still a very exciting time to be in Iowa (after the caucuses which catapulted Barack Obama into the limelight) and in America, although it is not yet totally clear if we will be witnessing change, hope, sleaze, corruption, apocalypse now…or all of the above. I am hopeful that this work, as well as my past and future endeavors, will focus the level of discourse in our country upon the personal, philosophical, psychological and professional aspects of life and guide us away from excessive materialism, power politics and egocentric narcissism (as I write this, Eliot Spitzer has just resigned from the Governorship of New York State for reasons now known by the entire free world and his replacement has announced a series of problems of his own).

To my dear friends, brilliant colleagues, students and mentors who have contributed many chapters to this publication, you have done a great deal indeed for our fellow citizens who have been clamoring for a book such as this. Each chapter speaks for itself and presents a unique aspect of the rich and profound approach to life known as "existentialism." Some chapters are extremely personal, others quite professional, political or academic. Some represent a mixture of all of the above approaches. Some are professionally edited, others we just decided to "let 'em ride."

To all of those who have already acquired this work, or who may do so in the future, thank you in advance for giving us this opportunity to have our voices heard- perhaps for one last and glorious time. If there's one great aspect left in America, it's the God-given and governmentally protected right to be heard- over and over and over again. God Bless America, land that we all still love…warts and all.

Sincerely yours,

Richard V. Campagna, Iowa City, 3/15/08

1. Not All Who Wander Are Lost!

by Sarah M. Haaf

Who am I? This is one of the most difficult questions I have ever encountered. I can tell you who I should be. I can tell you who I want to be. I can even tell you who I'm not. Yet, I still pose the question: who am I? Well, I *am* someone who poses this question. Life for me feels like a child's playground. Without caution, one could disregard nature's laws, and fall-perhaps falling hard. However, with too much caution, one might never realize their own courage and strength after reaching the top of the bars.

Hearing your name in conjunction with existentialism is a little daunting. All sorts of emotions swirl in your filtered mind. Being a woman at the tender age of 26, I am in constant reminder of my youth; whether it is in reference to my 'silly' behavior, excuses for my lifestyle or encouragement for my shortcomings. For those who have encountered wisdom, it is tranquil reassurance. 'Forge ahead—continue your path and you will be a success.' But what is success, and who defines it? Most importantly, why am I consumed with the need to have it?

Personal development oftentimes arranges itself around personal crisis. My crisis began when I was 17. I wish my story was more glamorous, but in reality, it is quite ordinary. Perhaps that is why I was chosen by my mentor, Richard Campagna, to tell it. Thru the guidance of my parochial school advisors, as well as my idealistic faith, I had planned my life down to the millisecond. Even then, I was going 'against the grain', pursuing an acting career in both theater and film, I was also playing along the path of prearranged acceptance. I had been verbally accepted at the college of my choice, and I felt I was on my way. I would be moving to Boston—my dream college town—away from everything I knew of Iowa. It was when I received my rejection letter from this very same school that my surrounding walls melted into grey waves. Not long thereafter, the boy I discovered puppy love with told me he was moving to Germany— away from me and any possible future developments in our relationship. Two 'Dear John' letters, two slaps of rejection— propelled me into a state of mental and emotional disarray.

A year of ups and downs followed—decisions were made, decisions were lost. I finally gathered up enough muster to tell my parents I would be taking a year off from school. The first pangs of disappointment rolled around in their eyes. I felt both as a soldier, preparing for a homeland security battle, as well as a wounded victim, unaware of who would protect me. Both my pride and my resolution drove my steadfast declaration. What followed this decision was a year full of firsts. Many of these firsts were learning experiences as well as traps into a life that began to feel foreign. I began to see someone in the mirror I did not recognize. Whatever 'sunshine' that once directed my face now seemed to shift into the grayness of 'real world' life, and with that, disappointment of my own. I became lost in a man whom I loved as well as hated. I went back to school, regretful of every step, with the exception of my class on Eastern Religions and Philosophy. I was introduced to a Theater Company which was my only solitude; however I became so self conscious that I was attacking my own work. I had to get away. I had to go somewhere that I didn't know. I decided

Minneapolis was a safe first step—said I was moving there, and two weeks later, I was unpacking in my new apartment.

Life choices are the only way for one to become reconnected to one's spirit. I cannot say whether my move to Minneapolis was a 'smart decision' in the eye of success or not, but I can say that what I learned there was invaluable. I relearned how to breathe. I met new types of people, I became conscious of the surrounding world, and I learned how to be thankful for the things I was given, and the things I worked hard to achieve. With all of these gifts, I was allotted the most important of my life. I became more aware of my existence—how I am affected by others, and how I affect others. I saw fragments of my optimistic self, and for the first time, I was taking responsibility for my placement. I no longer felt that I was floating on some wave that formed before I entered the pool. I saw how making decisions about what I wanted, and striving every moment to accomplish these goals, rendered the universe over to my desires. It was never easy—but I somehow found the money I needed, and a way into which I could step into my own dreams. I was soon to be moving to New York to study acting.

New York. . .

The first day in New York's West Village by myself, I took a long and enchanting walk. At this point, I was still too afraid to ride the subway on my own, but thankfully I moved in the early days of summer, and the city beckoned me to explore it. I had never lived in a place where I knew no one. Millions of strangers felt more comforting to me than handfuls of close friends. I retraced the steps of countless others before me. I became alive with the colors, the sounds, and the smells of New York City. I began carrying a journal everywhere with me. I found cafes and small used book shops that smelled of history. Music danced with the wind, and bakeries highlighted street corners. Humor was represented in all aspects of New York life; the aroma on the streets, a mixture of restaurant delicacies and urine. Everything charmed me. A middle aged gay couple walked the streets hand in hand—both men well above six feet tall and covered in tattoos and leather. Small dogs were decorated by designers that I had never dreamed of being able to afford for myself. Children darted around me, giggling and talking of foreign affairs. The harbor's waters rested only three blocks from my caged apartment, allowing snapshot views. The Statue of Liberty became more meaningful than I ever imagined, the way a child finally notices how a remote control works. Everything I saw impelled me to a state of awe, and also a sense of disappointment. The glamour I had seen on T.V. and in movies was nothing of the real New York. Descriptions held truer to her sense: New York really was a beating heart—but like most hearts, she has her ups and downs.

I started acting school a month after I moved to the city. I was anxious during every step of my new adventure. Genuine smiles relaxed me into most situations, but those were few and far between. I looked around the room during my initial interview, feeling more foreign than the world citizens sitting across from me. I was unique with my American accent, and my blonde hair and blue eyes seemed the most boring traits my parents could have passed on to me. I became easily engaged in the multitude of accents, and fascinated with the realization that all my self-imposed importance was actually meaningless. I had conjured my life dreams into something I had highly overrated. Thankfully, I was able to see more than my focused fairytale, and engaged in another awakening experience. I learned the most important lesson of all: I had always known the answers, but that I had to break down my path to discovery. I had to relearn how to think, how to see, hear, smell, taste, and touch the world around me. I had to find out that I needn't seek answers anywhere else than where they had always been-inside of me.

I seemed to be making the right choices, and became only more encouraged when Richard would visit New York. I eagerly accepted every invitation for breakfast or lunch. Although I would become discouraged by my lack of work, I relished advice from this seasoned advocate of life—and was delighted that his 'gut feeling' complemented ideas and quests I had independently sought. He and a select few charged me to better myself, and to continue to deny the outline I had scripted for my life. His guidance felt like reassurance for what I knew—that living my life had to come from myself. I had to continue to live my life the way I felt most rightly fit me, no matter what others had intended for me.

Somehow, my amazing gift of awareness eventually left me more desperate to find what I was seeking—and more confused on what I wanted in life. New York began as a gateway to freedom, and became a prison of tall buildings, and congested lungs. My creativity was not just slowed—it was catapulted into a state of nothingness. It no longer existed. My understanding of my entire existence seemed to hang in the bellows of an essential decision. Did I stay and continue on, hoping to encounter a sign from the heavens above, or did I leave and start over again? Neither option felt desirable, but my prolonged contemplation was wearing me thin. I had to choose, or I would fall, and fall hard. One night I closed my eyes and decided to meditate on it as I slept. This was one of the few nights in my life I did not remember my dreams—but I will never forget awakening from that particular slumber. I called my father the moment I opened my eyes and said "Daddy, I'm coming home". Two weeks later, he was there, packing me into his familiar Jeep—and we headed west. I cried as I watched the city become smaller in my rear view mirror. He didn't say anything —and I thanked him with my silence. He might not have understood that I was leaving the love of my life—but he knew me well enough to know that all great things in my life—lead me to tears.

Heading West . . .

As we drove into Iowa I was washed with familiar sights and smells, but now they all seemed to be continuous canvases of washboard white. Nothing seemed to engage me; only the silence let me close my eyes. My entire drive from the east coast was spent questioning my decision. I was in an internal battle for my soul. My father's presence calmed me enough to allow me to rest. I spent the next two months planning my retreat. I excused my move home by telling myself I was home for only a few months just to make enough money to get me towards my next goal. I couldn't let the idea of Iowa sit with me long enough to pardon it. Slowly, I eased out of my own denial. I was responsible for my own placement. I had run out of money and out of emotional energy to support my own path. I needed to recoup, I just needed a reason to do it. Then, early one morning, I got my reason.

My father's heart stopped beating around 8:30 am on a Thursday. It had been less than an hour from when we first called the paramedics, to when his time of death was declared. I sat on the floor next to his cooling body for hours. I held his large bear paw of a hand in mine, hoping for some miracle to bring a sign of life. It never came. And slowly with his body, my life drained from me. I felt like a shell of myself—and work became only a break from a bottle of wine, or endless hours of sleepless paralysis. My canvas was now covered in blood stained tears. My path had become a slow struggle to recover from pressed degeneration.

The year that followed is a blur of visions. I made important connections and friendships, and I never stopped planning where I would be going next, but the thought of leaving exhausted me. I knew I couldn't stay, but the act of leaving was too much for my frail spirit to endure. I went in circles, trying to sort through the puzzle I had begun. I didn't want to leave my now widowed mother, nor my sister and her new son. We were all sharing the same lung and I didn't know how to be separated from them. A friend from New York called me one random night, and told me he felt I was slowly quitting my dream. He knew I no longer felt acting was important. I denied it then, but after a while, I saw that he was right. I felt guilty for wanting to continue on with my dreams, when my father's had been cut short.

Although college had failed my aspirations during the first attempt, I danced around the idea of going back to school. Yet every time I researched subjects of study, I felt a pang in my stomach. I knew I was being disloyal and non-genuine to myself. I placed myself around others that had followed a very different path than I had. I looked up to them for allowing themselves a lack of empathy. They challenged my beliefs and were supportive of my pondering ways. They were forward looking thinkers that didn't waste time searching; they acted. They forced me to want to act. I soon realized their path was not for me. Then one night, I picked up my journal again. I locked myself in a room with a computer, and listened to music. I rented international and independent films. I learned how to cook. I made a list of all the things I wanted to do in life—and I made a special note of things I had accomplished that were on my list previously.

A few months went by and I began healing from my previously described fall. I decided to reach high and explore possibilities for a move to Europe—another lifelong dream. I began the paperwork and made contacts overseas. Life started to look attractive again. I started a new job, and with the New Year, my mother gifted me a weeklong trip to California. While I was there, she shared with me the final thought my father had shared with her about me: "He had to find a way to get me to California." His stated desire only supported the decision I had made the moment I stepped out into the California sunshine. I needed to come here, at least for a little while. Again Richard stamped my life by offering me an opportunity that would enhance my ability to make a short term move to a new home. I called my manager at work, and gave her the date of my final work day. I would be in Northern California in less than three months.

As I am writing this, I am in my final few weeks before I depart for California. The snow still falls here on the Iowa corn-fields. I have found a place of peace and love during my stay in Iowa. I have fallen in love again with my home, and now that I am recharged with a little sunshine, I plan my trip to the West Coast with a little of the gusto I once felt in my life. My mother, sister, nephew and I are all breathing on our own again, though our time spent together has brought us closer than we had ever predicted we could be. We realize we all have our own paths—our own stories to create and keep re-creating. I have no idea how long I will be in California. I do not know if I will make it to Europe. I hope I do. My father will have been gone for two years in August of 2008. I left New York in May of 2006. This was only a small sliver of my life, not even close to the eventual icing on the cake...

Sarah Michal Haaf is a remarkable, dedicated young actress, writer and director. She also juggles careers in the hospitality and beauty/health care industries. Her exuberance, organizational skills and 'existential optimism' have taken her from her place of birth (Iowa City) to Minneapolis, New York City and Northern California, where she currently resides. She is the proud daughter of Mary and Dan Haaf, from whom she learned many of the existentialist principles and approaches developed in the foregoing chapter.

2. The Moral Necessity of Personal Freedom

by Peter Catsimpiris

Introduction

Existential philosophy identifies the individual human person as the fundamental metaphysical unit in the universe and his or her free will as the fountainhead of all value. It is by this same consummate concern for personal freedom that Libertarian political philosophy is readily seen as a sympathetic and even complementary endeavor; political philosophy, as a subset of ethics, concerns at its core our individual actions, the restrictions that ought (or ought not) to be placed on those actions, and, perhaps most critically, *whence* such restrictions ought to stem. If, as Sartre contended, our bedrock human dignity and identity is founded in the very pursuit of our individual free wills, it is clear that our primary political goal must then be to obliterate any trace of the coercion of individual human persons from the edifice of civilization; and so the link between Existentialism and Libertarianism would seem inevitable.

Many ingenious, passionate, and hallowed arguments for the Libertarian worldview have been proffered over the centuries, from Lao Tzu to Milton Friedman and beyond. The following chapter will neither resurrect nor despoil any of these, nor will it establish its assertions upon the common assumptions of Existential philosophy or the classics of Libertarian thought, solid foundation though they be; rather, what follows is a brash effort to justify the clarion call of political liberty still ringing through the ages *from first principles*, based solely upon the respective definitions of ethics and the human will. Thus here we bow deeply to our forbears in recognition of their Herculean accomplishments and submit the following with a humble prayer for success or else the charity of pardon.

I.

In concerning ourselves with the constitution of the ideal state, and thereby the "oughts" specifically of the political realm—e.g., "how *ought* a just government be constituted?" or, "how *ought* individuals treat one another?"—we are interested ultimately in the will of the rational being. Any "ought," in the final analysis, boils down to the attempt of one mind to provide *reasons* for or against action to another in terms it itself finds convincing and by which it expects to convince the other. As such, any "ought" begs a "why," which regress must finally terminate in an object of the common will of at least these two minds. Take for instance a mother telling her son that he "ought to do his homework." This "ought" begs a "why," which will uncover its ultimate determining ground—in this case, perhaps "because doing so will help you get into college"—in an object of the will positing the "ought" which is expected also to be an object of the will asked to heed that "ought." There are thus such "oughts" that will be unconvincing. Take for example a vigilant onlooker chiding a would-be arsonist and telling him he "oughn't play with matches" for fear he might start a fire. Ultimately, if the object of the will underlying any "ought" is not deemed valuable by the responding party, he has not been given sufficient reason to act as asked.

As Immanuel Kant points out in his *Groundwork of the Metaphysics of Morals*, however, the "oughts" of the moral realm are presumed to carry universal weight and validity—i.e., to command action of all rational beings regardless of their other inclinations or commitments; insofar as they are really moral "oughts," they must command *categorically* and without exception—they must provide sufficient reasons for action to any and all possible rational beings capable of determining their own wills and acting upon them, *merely insofar* as they are such beings.

We are aiming to establish laws that are to delimit the actions of *all* individual rational beings, and also to which any of them, insofar as they are willing to reason about the subject merely *as rational beings* (and without thought of contingent facts about themselves such as inclinations) can assent, and thus in fact *will*[1]. As Kant describes it, the project of ethics is thus the *self-governance* of the action of the rational being—i.e., *by his or her very own reason*. And so the categorical nature of moral laws—i.e., their ability to command everyone everywhere—must derive from indisputable facts about the nature of reason and the rational being which do not vary across the set of all possible agents.

Kant's great insight is thus that in order for any "ought" to command *categorically*, it must have as its basis not some outcome a given rational being may (or may not) himself will, but rather something valued by a rational being absolutely and without exception *by definition* and *a priori*, merely insofar as he or she is a rational being. While Kant posits his own such value standard and goes on to derive from it the tenets of his moral theory, we will diverge from his approach in the next section

[1] If such absolutely commanding moral laws should be found to exist which delimit human interaction, any government (itself merely a collection of individuals) would also be bound to obey them, and therefore not to establish policies which violate them.

(owing to our different purposes) and argue for "the fundamental freedom of the individual rational being to determine and to act upon his or her own will free from coercion" as one such value held absolutely by all rational beings, and upon which we will establish the moral-political stipulations of libertarianism as commanding *categorically*.

II[2]

Merely insofar as I have a will, I must will my own freedom, with freedom defined as broadly as possible—i.e., "the absence of any obstacle to the achievement of one's will." In order to demonstrate this, we need only to consider the possibility of willing its opposite—i.e., the *frustration* of my will—and show this to be absurd. To begin, it is impossible *a priori* for any person to will the frustration of his or her own will, since any object of a will (in this case, "the frustration of one's own will") is trivially in accordance with that will, and so its obtaining cannot possibly violate the very will of which it itself is an object.

Even if we should erect some standard beyond our own will whose fulfillment we desire even in the event that it should conflict with our own desires at a given time—e.g., we might hope that "God's will be done" or "my wife's will be done"—we are nonetheless committed to the absolute achievement of our *own* will, given that it is in fact our own will which has posited this external standard. Simply put, insofar as I will the achievement of anything at all, since that state of affairs *must* thereby be an object of my will, I am also committed to the absolute achievement of my will *per se*, and thereby to the absence of all obstacles in its pursuit—i.e., my *freedom*.

As such, the personal freedom of each individual rational

---

[2] I am greatly indebted to Ryan Mason for hours spent developing and criticizing the ideas in this section with me.

being possessing a will is in fact of *ultimate* value to that individual, as no other value can supersede it. And given the aforementioned categorical impossibility of a person willing the curtailment of his or her own freedom, coinciding with that value is in fact both a necessary and sufficient condition for anything to be of value to that individual at all.

While it is clear that each individual must categorically and *a priori* will his or her own freedom, the question remains whether we must all willingly *restrain* our own action whenever conflicts between various wills should arise; that is, we still need an account of why it is that all of us as rational beings are committed not only to the preservation of our own freedom, but in fact to that of others as well. To begin, as we recall from section I above, any moral "ought" must command categorically, and so it must be rooted in some object of the will of a rational being *as such*—that is, something that any and all rational beings, merely insofar as they are such beings, must will. A technique[3] to ascertain those objects of the will of a rational being *as such* which offers itself to us here is that of considering some objective observer, stripped of all personality, inclinations, desires, etc.—i.e., devoid of any and all objects of a will which are not necessary *a priori* for each and every rational being to hold.

In consideration of such an objective observer, it is quite certain that, in the event of a conflict between my will and that of another, any object of *my* will cannot in any way carry more weight for the objective observer than any object of *anyone else's* will. To see why this is the case, imagine my opponent in any such conflict to be a perfectly rational, well-meaning individual, but nonetheless interested in picking the same apple from an orchard that I wish to pick. If we are both dead set on picking that apple, and truly will to eat it, it seems on face that neither

---

[3] I am here also indebted to Immanuel Kant in his Groundwork of the Metaphysics of Morals. A similar Kantian technique is also employed by John Rawls in A Theory of Justice, although to far different ends.

of us can provide *objective* reasons to the other to restrain his own action and to allow the other's will to be achieved and thereby for his or her freedom to remain inviolate. This is because the objective observer is incapable of distinguishing between my will and the will of my opponent in the event of such a conflict, since the objects of our respective wills are ultimately of value to each of us for exactly the same reason— namely, their being a stipulation of our respective wills; as such, either outcome—i.e., my eating the apple or my opponent's eating the apple—would seemingly violate the freedom of one individual for the sake of the other, making it impossible for the objective observer to adjudicate in favor of either. And so, since our *objective* observer cannot make an objective decision, it seems that each of us remains, at least at this point, committed only to *his or her own* freedom.

As we recall, only a standard necessarily willed by any and all rational beings merely insofar as they have wills can possibly come under the consideration of the objective observer when he or she is asked to resolve such disputes. As such, any standard that would proceed only from a personal will (which of course the objective observer by definition does not even possess) can thus not possibly be used as a basis for the adjudication of such conflicts by recourse to moral "oughts." And so even defaulting on judgment for the objective observer is fundamentally impossible: simply put, a degeneration of such disputes into "might makes right" situations would ultimately be absurd, since it suggests the *a posteriori*, contingent happenstance of power as the basis of the relative value of certain outcomes and the achievement of one will over another, which is certainly not *a priori* desirable by the rational being as such.[4]

We now realize that a stalemate in the eyes of the objective

---

[4] A utilitarian adjudication of disputes is likewise dismissed by this point, along with any other theory of value not provable on a priori grounds and thereby not convincing to the objective observer.

observer (the inevitable result of which would be a "might makes right" adjudication of such disputes) is unacceptable, and so it is critical that we find some moral standard of judgment to which all of us rational beings can (and must) assent in the event of a conflict between wills. In pursuit of this, the only thing both parties seem obliged to agree upon *a priori* is the ultimate value of their own respective freedoms. Now if it is the case, as we've shown above, that his or her own personal freedom is of *a priori* importance to any individual rational being merely insofar as he or she is a rational being, it must also be the case, as we've shown in section I, that the preservation of freedom *per se* is of *a priori* value to the objective observer, the content of whose will is in fact identical with all *a priori* willings of actual rational beings. The difference, however, is that the objective observer can possess no *personal* will, and so has no basis to value the freedom of one individual over another, but is nonetheless committed to the value of personal freedom *per se*, adjudging it of equal value regardless of whose it is due to the lack of any possible *a priori* standard by which to value the freedom of one over another. More starkly, if I am to find *my* freedom to be of categorical importance merely on the basis that I myself am "a rational being possessing a will," it is clear that I am logically obligated to approve of the induction of the freedom of all "rational beings possessing a will" (i.e., freedom *per se*) as of objective categorical value to all "rational beings possessing a will."

To further illustrate that this is the case, we need only to employ another *reductio ad absurdum*. If an objective observer could possibly value something higher than personal freedom *per se*, and consequently rule in favor of violating an individual's freedom for the sake of some other value in the event of a conflict, he or she would be forced into suggesting a supposedly moral (and therefore *categorical*) "ought" to an individual, the accomplishment of which that individual could not possibly will, since it would violate his or her own freedom. This, given our very definition of morality in section I as what must be always and everywhere willed by rational beings, is an absurdity, and so we have shown that the objective observer must ineluctably value the preservation of freedom *per se* above all else.

We've thus shown that in cases where two individuals are at loggerheads, and regular avenues of resolving disputes between them have been exhausted to no avail—e.g., negotiation, trade, or any other means of assimilating the two individual wills—the objective observer and therefore our collective moral compass will always point to the preservation of the freedom of one individual as more valuable than anything else.[5] Several questions now present themselves: what about cases of freedom vs. freedom: have we not already eliminated from the realm of possibility an objective observer valuing the freedom of one individual over that of another? And further, is it not the case that in all such conflicts between wills, both individuals' freedom is at stake, given our broad definition of freedom as "the absence of any obstacle to the achievement of one's will"?

[5] This is not to say that there might not be further moral obligations and duties required of an individual merely insofar as he or she possess a rational will, but only that one such absolute and inviolable obligation, regardless of other ends or inclinations, is that he or she respect the freedom of others. Furthermore, even if we could argue that there were other things necessary to will *a priori* and so which command our action categorically, their *enforcement* in violation of individual freedom could never be considered *morally necessary* due to the fact that in a world of just one person, said enforcement would be impossible, resulting in a world that is trivially immoral—something we can certainly never countenance!

III.

We might make inroads into answering these questions by resort to a thought experiment whose form has been current at least since Locke's *Two Treatises*, especially in justifying a Libertarian type of political organization—namely, consideration of a possible "state of nature."

In a situation in which there were only one person with a will on this earth, the violation of freedom would be a non-concept. Since, as shown in section II, the will cannot violate its own freedom, and it is also only to a will that the impossibility and impropriety of willing the violation of any other rational being's will pertains, our single earthly denizen would neither be able to violate his or her own freedom, nor would he or she in fact have it violated by the outside world, which, by virtue of its possessing no will, could not be restrained in its operations by any reasons whatsoever, much less reasons that apply only to possessors of a will. Thus, such an individual would in fact be at no risk of having his or her freedom violated, and consequently would possess all the security in his or her life, liberty and person, and property to which he or she is entitled.

As such, to be denied what nature herself would have denied one is *in a no way* a violation of one's freedom. On the other hand, to be denied what nature would have allowed one is an encroachment (however small it might be) upon the will of that individual, and therefore quite clearly a violation of his or her freedom by another person endowed with a rational will. The oft-mentioned notions of positive and negative rights derive directly from this analysis: a negative right is a claim to something nature herself would never have denied an individual; whereas positive rights imply a claim to something earmarked by nature for *another* individual, and so something which would have been denied by nature to the individual making the claim.

As we integrate such lone persons into a society of two or more, certain forms of coercion by one on another are thus quite easy to identify, as they clearly involve one person employing force to determine the other's action—i.e., a granting of positive rights over negative rights, and thereby a denial of freedom. In cases of murder, assault, kidnapping, and other such blatant violations[6] upon the person and will of another, the respective identities of the party doing the coercing and the party being coerced are as readily apparent as the occurrence of the coercion itself—the victim would surely be secure from all such infringement on their will in a world without any other human beings, and so the aggressor has without any question violated the victim's freedom.

Further, since it is clear that in a state of nature we cannot fail to obtain all to which we are entitled, we can obviously have no *right* or claim to any property we do not ourselves produce. As such, the holding of property by others can in no way be considered theft of "potential property" from ourselves, as we in fact have no claim on it given that, since we did not ourselves produce[7] it, nature would have similarly denied it to us, and so our inability to possess it can in no way be considered coercion. On the other hand, since the person who produces the property he or she owns would of course be absolutely secure in its possession in a state of nature, any potential thief would of course violate the freedom of such a victim.

But how are we to deal with property situations that are more ambiguous, such as the acquisition of the rights to natural resources, or other *procured* rather than *produced* property? And what of property that is technically self-produced, but only

[6] Included in this category would of course be any attempt to force a lifestyle or other purely personal decision upon an individual.

[7] In a market economy, "production" of property takes many forms and is thus ultimately to be ascertained by a lack of force and a presence of either free trade or literal production as the means of acquisition for said property.

by means of a process involving other people, who would certainly have been absent in a state of nature?

Since what we are eliminating from human interaction is the willful violation of freedom, we can argue for the "inductive purity" of property as yielding a right to its possessor to own it, which means nothing other than a negative claim on the action of all other individuals "not to coerce it out of his or her possession." In other words, property acquired through means excluding the coercion of others is property to which its owner has a rightful claim, which not only eliminates on face the possibility of such a property owner's coercion of others by holding onto his or her own property, but in fact marks out the forcible coercion of that property out of its present owner's possession as categorically unacceptable—again, it would obviously be an assault on his or her freedom, whereas his or her possession of that property is in no way an infringement on the freedom of another, who could not possibly have any claim to it.

But how do we define an "inductively pure" process? In doing so, it will be necessary for us only to distinguish between coercion and negotiation—any process involving coercion lacks the inductive purity necessary to bequeath inviolable negative rights to the possessor of certain property, whereas a process of acquisition involving *anything but coercion*, including personal labor, trade, or negotiation, is granted inductive purity and with it the seal of approval of our objective observer. So what is the fundamental difference between coercion and negotiation?

Coercion is involved in any process of acquisition of property wherein the acquiring party pursues or threatens infringement on the negative rights of another. Take for example the difference between the statements: "I'll cut your throat if you don't give me your car keys," and "I won't help you with your homework if you don't pay me ten dollars." In the first statement, the party intent on transaction has actually passed into the realm of coercion insofar as he or she is threatening to act in a way that violates the freedom of the other party in trespassing upon those things to which that person has a negative right bestowed by the state of nature and a process of inductive purity—i.e., in the example, his or her very life. On the contrary, in the second statement the party intent on transaction is not in any way violating the will of the respondent party, since he or she is threatening only to exercise control over aspects of his or her own "domain"—that is, those things over which he or she has a negative right—i.e., in the example, his or her own time and labor.

IV.

Through sections II and III, we have demonstrated that it is categorically immoral for any person to violate the freedom of any other; thus, any government trespassing on the negative rights of any individual at any time, as itself metaphysically nothing greater than a collection of individuals, is in fact unwillable and therefore immoral. The question thus arises as to the very possibility of establishing a moral government if in fact said government is incapable of initiating force against citizens or outsiders, and thereby *seemingly* incapable even of sustaining itself by levying taxes, raising an armed police force, or waging war.

While the problem of justifying the existence of government in the face of the ethical analysis presented in the preceding sections of this chapter might cast a monolithic shadow, we can readily break the question down into several smaller issues. To begin with, we might divide the matter in two by outlining the legitimate functions[8] of a government and then moving on

---

[8] We must remember that, upon later philosophical investigation into the *a priori* conditions of the will as such, it is quite conceivable that some of the functions of government that may still seem legitimate per our analysis in sections I through III will turn out to be immoral (i.e., categorically unwillable). As such, those functions identified as legitimate in the following analysis are in fact only *potentially* legitimate, and not *necessarily* so.

to suggest the legitimate means of funding these legitimate functions.

First, let us consider the various functions we commonly associate with a government. In the modern welfare states that dominate our political era, we find the government assuming the sundry roles of social safety net, environmental protector, healthcare provider, guarantor of public safety and the common defense, educator of our children, general safety inspector, builder and maintainer of public works, retirement plan overseer, and defender of morals and culture, among numerous others. For our purposes, we'll divide these many offices into three primary categories: defense, services, and social engineering.

In the last of these categories falls any attempt of governments at any level to regulate the lives and lifestyles of its citizens. From laws prohibiting fornication to statues restricting speech, these legal endeavors to mandate what are often laudable morals or standards are in fact categorically unacceptable per our discussion in the preceding sections of this chapter. Simply put, any such program is an indisputable assault on the freedom of its subjects, and so no further analysis is here required to deny the just government any ability so to socially engineer.

In the second of these categories—i.e., services—fall any of the vast swathe of welfare programs founded to assist some segment of a population with living expenses, healthcare, etc— essentially, any program reducible to financial assistance from the government to citizens for any number of possible purposes. On face, such programs do not run into the same moral difficulties of the aforementioned category of social engineering, as assisting willing citizens with their finances *per se* is obviously not a violation of anybody's freedom. As such, the possibility of elimination of this category from the potential functions of a just government lies with the ancillary concern of funding —i.e., could we justify bankrolling such an elaborate system of handouts with coercive taxes and wealth redistribution? And so we will return to this category later, when we examine the means a government may take to fund its operations.

Finally, we must consider the category of defense, in which a military, police force, and even the entire criminal justice system and civil law courts can be placed—i.e., all functions of a government aimed at preserving and protecting the negative-right domains discussed in section III. Programs in this category conspicuously necessitate the use or threat of force for their very implementation, but, ideally, in the hopes of protecting rights and thereby freedom rather than violating them. This category of governmental function thus doubtless appears the most controversial based on our previous analysis.

To begin, it may turn out, upon further investigation into the *a priori* conditions of the rational will, that self-defense and the protection of one's own rights by force is unacceptable. Based upon the findings of sections I through III above, however, there is no reason to suggest that this is the case—i.e., insofar as one is using or threatening force in the *preservation* of an individual's negative rights rather than with an aim to *violate* them, one is not transgressing anyone's freedom and so is acting in a way that remains moral, at least per our earlier analysis. As such, it seems that a just government so constituted as to protect citizens from one another and outsiders by means of force or the threat of force is at no risk of immorality in virtue of this function of defense. And so the establishment of police forces at various levels from local to federal, a military marshaled to preserve the common defense, and a civil and criminal justice system founded on sound principles of jurisprudence grounded in the sanctity of personal freedom and individual rights is a thoroughly acceptable function of the ideal state.

At this point we might ask how a government would fund such a venture. In responding to this question we transition from our previous discussion of the legitimate *functions* of a just state to an investigation into the legitimate means of *funding* these endeavors. As with the case of welfare left previously unanswered, in funding defense, no doubt a wholly acceptable and even a laudable governmental operation, a state must take care not to violate personal freedom. The coercive taxes that typically serve as the means of providing the public fisc would appear to transgress the negative rights of citizens and thereby prove immoral.[9] This is no doubt the death knell of the welfare state—i.e., if indeed coercive taxes are an immoral means of funding such operations, it is difficult to see how they might be propagated at all, given that they are nothing more than a denuded redistribution of wealth from one individual or group to another. As for defense, however, it may well be possible for the state to seek funding in a way that does not violate personal freedom—e.g., by some sort of "user-fees."[10]

How *exactly* such a proposal might be fleshed out is largely irrelevant to our present purpose. Nonetheless, it is incumbent upon us to show that in fact *some* such avenue exists. In this pursuit there seems to be one particularly promising proposal. Suppose that in any civil case brought before a court of any level, from petty cases to multi-billion dollar liability cases affecting multinational corporations, a percentage of the penalty awarded the plaintiff were taken by the court as a fee, perhaps

[9] There may well be an argument for the imposition of coercive taxes, especially to fund the law courts and common defense, as wholly legitimate and in no way a violation of personal freedom. Such an argument might proceed along lines similar to the claim that, say, a dog owner is obliged to purchase a leash and collar for his or her pet as well as a fence around his or her property, since to fail to do so constitutes a real physical threat to neighbors and passersby. Such an argument will not be presented here due both to space considerations and the fact that the subsequently discussed method of user-fees is far more philosophically appealing for a number of reasons, especially insofar as it does not admit of the same obvious "slippery slope" objections one could levy against the former.

[10] Interesting discussions of related proposals can be found in Ayn Rand's *The Virtue of Selfishness*.

accompanied by an additional penalty assessed to the losing party.[11] Since this situation would be understood prior to the court's hearing the lawsuit, it need not trespass on any party's freedom, but is rather metaphysically identical to any fee due for service in the private sector. With an appropriately sized government, tens if not hundreds of times cheaper to operate than the monstrosities that currently swallow the wealth of nations, this windfall could suffice to fund not only the civil courts, but in fact the other legitimate defense functions of the state[12] as well.

Afterword

Numerous questions remain surrounding the constitution of the ideal state. How exactly do we delimit personal negative-right domains—i.e., is there any "right" way, *per se*, or is Herodotus right that "custom is king?" How exactly do we determine the size and form of legal penalties for various

---

[11] Assessing a penalty to a losing defendant would seem to be problematic, given that the defendant is likely compelled to appear in court against his or her wishes, and so does not in any way choose the situation. It seems clear, however, that the morality of such a proposal rests on the same account as the morality of the entire criminal justice system, which would impose penalties and punishments on unwilling parties. The justification for both would likely consist in indicating that the defendant in all such cases would have been determined to be a violator of negative rights and thereby personal freedom, and so in some sense his or her own domain would have "shrunk" as a result of his or her crimes, forcing upon him or her a moral obligation to ensure restitution, including funding the operations of the state which make that restitution possible. The exact argument for such a system I leave to future writers.

[12] The possibility of thus funding a comprehensive military might be dubious; as such, the imposition of spoils and tribute on defeated foes might supplement these funds, justified along lines presented in note 10. If this system were also found to be practically unfeasible, coercive taxes for the purposes of defense might be justified along lines presented in note 8.

crimes? How do we ensure that, so far as possible, the court system remains objective and infallible? The list goes on.

Nonetheless, in the preceding sections we have demonstrated quite a bit: first, that, regardless of what *else* we must will *a priori* merely insofar as we possess a rational will, it is clear that we must will the universal preservation of freedom, and that, as such, to violate the freedom of any individual anywhere is consummately immoral. Second, we've demonstrated through a "state of nature" analysis that the universal preservation of freedom is in fact attainable. Third, as a corollary, we've shown that a government violating personal freedom is subject to the same immorality as any individual daring the same trespass. And finally, we've argued for the legitimacy of the defense functions of the state and suggested legitimate avenues of funding these operations. Satisfied with our achievements but hoping for clarity on the myriad and sundry questions left unanswered, we quit the bench of philosophy and leave the rest for the far more capable minds peopling the ranks of the legal, political, and philosophical professions, some of which, we shall hope, share the Existential view of freedom and count themselves as friends of liberty.

Peter Catsimpiris is a 22 year old Senior at Brown University (Class of 2008) majoring in Philosophy and Classics. He is a rising star in the liberty movement and has distinguished himself while serving as President of Students for Liberty at Brown. He will be going on to work at McKinsey & Co. in New York City this fall. I am confident that his future will be bright and his personal, professional and political success(es) will inure to the benefit of all of humanity.

3. Existential Psychology

by Leann Gentry

As far back as I remember, I have lived my life in an existential fashion, although as a 9 year old obviously, I wasn't familiar with the term. Nonetheless, at that tender age, I quickly wore out my favorite T-shirt which had printed on it in BOLD letters: "NORMAL PEOPLE WORRY ME." I don't know why, nor which of my two parents planted the idea in my head, but I grew up with the notion that you should always be yourself, do it your own way and I have lived by this motto ever since.

It is true that other people called me weird (in a nice way of course) but I think they are the weird ones. Why wouldn't you want to live your life the way you wanted to? Isn't it silly and degrading to yourself to change any aspect of your behavior to fit someone else's ideal? Ignoring the negative comments and refusing to give up, I have tried to live my life by always doing what I wanted, no matter if society deemed it to be wrong or not. This novel approach could be said to be the basis of Existential Psychology. Existential psychologists believe that people need to get down to the core of their true selves. In order to be truly happy you must be living life as you want to, in a genuine mode.

Existential psychologists teach that there is no absolute right or wrong behavior, with the exception perhaps of the Ten Commandments. Since we are all different, how can we compare ourselves to one another? Perhaps the only really wrong thing you can do is to conform to someone else's standards and not live up to your full potential. We cannot live up to our full potential if we do not fully comprehend our existence and the shortness of it. An existentialist is someone who is trying to grasp the concept of their own existence and that of all of humanity. He or she wants to understand the why and how of existence on their own, in their own minds. An existentialist can also be said to be a person who has matured sufficiently to the point where they take responsibility for their own existence and make the most out of it. Existential psychotherapy is meant to get people to "step up to the plate," if they are having difficulty doing so on their own. People must seize control of their lives, face their particular existence and that of all of humanity at the same time. Then they must "make their lives happen." Since most people don't have this ability, this is where the existential therapist enters the scene.

Many peoples' lives are filled with boundless energy and activities, inter-actions with other people and mounting stress so they don't get the opportunity to ponder the vast nothingness of the universe and the miniscule role that each of us plays in same. We are so busy in the hustle and bustle of life and discharging our "daily responsibilities" that many of us don't get a chance to look away from it all and wonder if there really is a point to life. This is not to say that there is no option regarding the existence of a God in our universe; there are many existential philosophers and psychologists who fervently believe in God. Many hold a positive and spiritual view with regard to their existence, including but not limited to: Paul Tillich, who was a Christian theologian and philosopher, Rollo May, a psychologist, Soren Kierkegaard, a philosopher and Martin Buber who was a Jewish theologian and philosopher.

Despite the possibility of God's existence, we are thrust here on earth, in this world, with limitless possibilities. Just because most people work at 9-5 jobs and are busy raising families and participating in the popular culture doesn't mean that that's what we're supposed to do necessarily. An existential psychologist opens up this window of unfettered choice to his or her clients. They get people to try to determine their purpose on earth since amidst all of the hustle and bustle of life, we can very easily start living pointless, meaningless and unfulfilling lives. When you live such a life you contribute to a downward spiral of all of humanity in my view. Existential psychologists get their clients to realize and accept the fact that they exist in this world and that each one of us is just as qualified as a human being as is any other human being.

It was a most opportune moment in my life to have been asked to write this chapter. I didn't know it at the time, but I have recently gone through my own "existential" transformation. It started a year and a half ago and I think I know what triggered it.

Please join me in my recollections, which I hope are instructive:

It started about a year and a half ago. I had just turned twenty years of age and had my mind set on someone...looking forward to seeing him every single day and probably thought about him every single hour. One thing led to another and I ultimately realized that he didn't feel the same way I did. This "constant" in my life was pulled out from underneath me. It represented a huge surprise and everything I had ever thought before was now questionable to me. My entire future was now blank. Much of my past existence also seemed empty and blank. I was faced with a new reality. Everything looked different to me. My mind opened up and I started seeing things from a different perspective. I wondered to myself: "What am I doing here?" I am just one of these other "people" and I live here in this town in Iowa. I felt such a deep and dark separation from my life because I had never before questioned why I was doing anything or if there is really any point to doing anything. I am now 22 and I feel as unimportant as a wildflower. It may sound disheartening but I am the happiest I have ever been in my entire life, thus far. I have never felt such a peace as I have achieved recently, knowing that my life will come to an end someday and when compared to the entire universe, I am quite miniscule. It now appears to me that there are informal stages that one will go through once you begin to grasp the essence of your existence. The existential psychologist is there to guide the patient/client and to keep him or her steady on this path; when you reach the end only then will you discover the incredible and overwhelming feeling of peace and freedom. The stages that you go through are vague and overlapping but there are definite and inevitable realizations that one achieves, while trying to wrestle down one's existence.

Firstly, whatever may be the cause, a particular triggering experience or simply upon reaching a certain age or maturity level, we reach the realization that we definitely DO exist in this world. Many psychologists refer to this as "self-actualization." Self actualization is difficult to define, as are most existentialist terms. My definition is that it is the process of becoming more of your true self. It is achieved by being able to look at yourself from an outside perspective but the key is to focus on one's own strengths and potential. While recognizing these positive aspects one doesn't ignore the reality of any possible "negative" aspects, but at this juncture you don't feel bad about your "negative" tendencies; they are just all a part of the complex human being that you are. Existential psychologists don't believe that any behavior is necessarily right or wrong, it is just different—it is the behavior that your percolating cerebral waters ultimately caused you to engage in. When you begin to self-actualize, you accept yourself for who you are and don't take things too seriously. You are no longer too hard on yourself. You realize that you are part of this human race and that you are just as important as any other human being.

This realization can be somewhat frightening at first. That is because you now have to step up and take responsibility for all of your actions; it now becomes your job to be all that you can be because now you know what you are capable of achieving. Once you have achieved this "outside-looking-in" view of yourself, you also reduce your own sense of self-importance. People who are important to you in your life could easily slip away due to moves, transfers or death. If you slipped away, certainly people would miss you but the world would go on. It always does. This realization can lead to feelings of loneliness because you face the fact that compared to the entire universe, you really don't matter...every person is disposable. Certainly we have friends and family but we are truly alone in the world. Our friends and family love us, but they are just other people like ourselves, wandering around and not knowing anything more than we know. No matter how long we have known someone, we are still responsible for ourselves since the other person may not always be there. When we come to grips with the foregoing...we have learned a great deal. We have accepted our existence, we have accepted ourselves and we have accepted the fact that we are easily disposable. We also begin to learn how short life is. We come to terms that we are like every other human being who has ever existed and we too will die someday. After we're gone, a few might remember you- what if they do, what if they don't?

At first, this is a rather sad realization; it is a positive thing for the existential therapist to bring these concepts to the minds of their patients. They strive to bring the patient into existential reality, whether it is nice or happy or not. But the reality of our lives is that they will end some day. This depressing thought, once fully accepted and embodied, will eventually cause you to cherish every single day of your life. Maybe we go somewhere afterwards, perhaps we don't. But we do know that our days here are limited and we can do with them absolutely whatever we choose. That is the ultimate freedom that the existentialist feels. As we age, we become more comfortable with these thoughts, thus leading ourselves to a peace of mind in which we consider our lives as a whole. We don't see things in terms of hours, how long we'll be at work today…or the squabble we just had with our spouse or significant other.

We see life as having a beginning, an ending and as an overall process. We begin to cherish the people with whom we have shared these beautiful times. Realizing that death is a cornerstone of life is an important process and it's best if accomplished earlier in life rather than later. Thinking about it often will help you to stop merely dealing with life in an unpleasant manner and to start seizing the day and making each one the best day of your life. I recently saw the movie, "Bucket List," an existentially oriented film, like many of Hollywood's recent productions. The characters portrayed by Jack Nicholson and Morgan Freeman were both dying of cancer and had less than a year to live so they decided to make the most of their time left. At one point in the movie, Morgan Freeman's character was reluctant to get a tattoo because he didn't want anything permanent. Nicholson's character replied: "What's permanent? We're gonna be dead in five minutes." This quote isn't exactly true for all of us but time does pass awfully quickly at times. In all of eternity, it's as if we were alive for only seconds. Existentialists realize this and therefore manifest a strong desire to live their lives to the fullest.

Why is it then that so many people don't live full and happy lives? What is it that holds them down? Existential therapy is aimed at freeing a person from the problem(s) that hold them back. The psychologist reminds their clients of existential truths and teaches them that their lives are their own responsibility. Even though they may have had problems in the recent past, there is no reason whatsoever they can't choose to make better decisions going forward. Some people need help in learning about their self-responsibility and need to focus on their own self-discovery processes or self-actualization. It eventually comes down to developing a "no-excuses" approach to life. One can see how many people wouldn't take kindly to this type of psychotherapy. It is too real for some people. Existential psychologists constantly remind their patients of where they live…in a place called reality. It is called Existential Psychology because it focuses on the existence of the "here and now." No matter what your genetic composition may be, your past, your hormonal state or even your subconscious, you don't have to do anything…and if you make a harmful choice, it's your fault. This form of therapy wipes away these "justifications" as to why you do the things you do. We have 100% control over our actions, our thoughts and our ultimate behaviors. This psychological approach puts YOU in the driver's seat.

It is both frightening and not very much fun to learn that we are who we are due to the choices that we consciously choose to make. It puts up a big, glaring mirror in front of the patient. Many people do not like to learn about their "existential" reality because they prefer to hear that they have some "disease" and they want to put their problems in someone else's hands to fix such for them. Believe me, it is much easier (and cheaper) to get real with yourself and just stop it. I think a lot of people, even some elderly, are emotionally immature in this respect.

It can be said that mainstream psychology itself has caused this epidemic of not taking the blame for our actions. Psychology has carried out much useful research but sometimes gets caught up in its own rigid, immutable diagnoses. Someone could assert: "Well my mom soothed my emotions as a child with food so now I am a compulsive overeater; it's my mom's fault I'm like this and I will be overweight for the rest of my life." That's just like saying something as absurd as: "Well Bob left a nail in the driveway so now my tire is flat; it's Bob's fault my car is unusable and now I can't use this car for the rest of my life." Sounds pretty absurd—but the parallel is clear to me. Just because something is broken doesn't give us the justification to just give up. Let's try and fix it. Things get broken. We all have things that cause us problems so you now know you can deal with it. Things such as our subconscious thoughts, our past and our genetics are not driving immutable forces. Your driving force is your mind at this moment...and the next moment... and each and every moment for the rest of your life. You are free to choose anything, everything or nothing and free to change your choice patterns at any moment in time.

Many people have questioned why we choose anything at all? If it is not our subconscious or our hidden sexual desires, what is in fact the driving force that makes us choose anything? There exists a theory that contends that there are two driving forces behind why we do anything. Either "Existential Anxiety" or "Existential Freedom." These two are quite the opposite of each other yet they can be closely intertwined. I personally believe that there is a process that one must go through in order to feel "Existential Freedom." One must deal with this and learn to overcome and accept the anxieties and wonders of our existence. Existential Anxiety is the anxiety that is felt almost naturally and one that can cause much disruption in your emotional well-being if not handled properly.

But such disruption need not be long-lived if you choose not to ignore it but to sort through it and deal with the consequences thereof. It is when a person realizes that they are alone in the world, that they cannot entirely share their exact experiences with another person, that the bell goes off. Anxiety is also caused by the realization that our lives will end someday. When we realize this, we seek some sort of constant in life, something to grasp onto and hold onto. We seek something that grounds us to the earth.

For me, when I was going through my period of "Existential Anguish" I realized that my only constant in life is my family because they will always be my family (although they will not always be here). Nothing can change that fact. We need some sort of grounding in this world so we don't get hopelessly lost in the nothingness. Thus, we make decisions that will help us feel comfortable, alive and connected.

While experiencing Existential Anxiety, one can be in constant fear of the reality of death or the fact that we could be struck with a horrible illness at any moment, because such is the naked truth. This is a very sad and disconcerting realization. It is sad initially but eventually we all learn to integrate all of the foregoing and to appreciate moments shared with our loved ones. These shared experiences are part of each participating party's individuality. Although each of these truths can seem scary and depressing, once they are accepted, we can begin to be moved by the second driving force which is "Existential Freedom." Existential Freedom is part of self discovery. Once you get past the anguish and finally accept reality for what it is, you begin to realize how short life is and you learn that you have freedom of choice. One day you can choose to be happy and work hard and the next day you can choose to mock and despise everything and try to see what little amount of work you can do to get by. Every day you can choose to be who you are. This makes life very fun and interesting. We continue to live the realization that we are here for a short while and that life is to be explored and experienced, not cursed and feared.

It is within this freedom that we can sit back and observe as well. Likewise, we can experiment with our lives. There is no absolute right or wrong, just different choices with different outcomes. You can choose to rob a bank and you may end up in jail for 20+ years and when you get out you can choose to have an organic farm and live with monks and meditate all day while donating all your money and belongings to charity. And when you are done with that you can go rob a bank again for some excitement! When you are amidst all of this freedom you view life as if you are in a movie. If some not so great things happen, it's okay since it's just all part of the beauty and non-predictability of this thing called "life."

Essentially, Existential Psychology tries to get people to look at themselves as a whole and is cognizant of the fact that that are many different levels of self-awareness. It also teaches people that they have free will by reminding them that they aren't just observing their lives as things "happen" to them; they are not the helpless playthings of history. Rather, they are active participants who control the outcome of their lives and they should live as authentically as possible. It also ensures that everyone's life does have a meaning, that we are all part of the human race and we all have something to contribute and therefore should contribute, on an ongoing basis.

We are continually changing and exploring our existence to become better human beings. Many of us live in life-long self-deception, hiding from the truths of the world and of our own personal responsibility. The psychologist works at getting people to face the realities of their lives and life in general, rather than withdrawing and retreating from them (I guess I still have some serious work to do; don't we all?). The psychologist does her best to immerse herself into the life of the patient. She wants to know about the patient's past, what they do on a daily basis and the like. In order to guide the patient on his journey towards existential awareness, she must fully understand what it is like to be the patient. She works alongside them and it is her job to keep an open mind and accept any differing beliefs or approaches patients may have. She also focuses on what matters most to the client and is serious about any issue they may present. The way I see it is that the Existential Psychologist must put up a mirror to the life of the patient/client and let him or her know that they are very important as human beings and that they are important members of society. The psychologist pounds home the fact that each patient exists and matters in the course of human history. Any particular issue that the client may have is one that needs to be addressed and dealt with; the patient must listen to the voice inside of himself and then live and act accordingly.

The practice of using Existentialism as a therapeutic approach emerged from the philosophies of European existentialists such as Kierkegaard, Nietzsche, Heidegger, Sartre and Husserl. Ludwig Binswanger is one of the first to use existentialist theories with his therapy. He was a psychiatrist who was born in Kreuzlingen, Switzerland in 1881 and lived by means of his writings and his scholarship until his death in 1966. He studied under Carl Jung and was a lifelong friend of Sigmund Freud. His most famous subject was the notable Ellen West who was a very curious and troubled woman who suffered from Anorexia Nervosa. Binswanger demonstrates a very logical way of classifying everything he does. Explaining the concept of loneliness he states: "Loneliness is an unhappy compound of having lost one's point of reference, of suffering the fate of individual and collective discontinuity and of living through or dying from a crisis of identity to the point of alienation of one's self."

Another pioneer of Existential Therapy was Victor Frankl. He followed Heidegger's existential theories and put them to great use in his logotherapy. He was born in Vienna in 1905 and lived until 1992. He developed an existentially inspired mode of therapy known as Logo Therapy. Logos means meaning. It should be noted that Frankl was in a Nazi concentration camp for 3 years, where he developed the concept of logotherapy. He noticed that the prisoners most likely to survive were those who had a sense of meaning and purpose; they had something in the future upon which they were focused and they looked forward to it. In his own words: "Everyone has his own specific vocation or mission in life; everyone must carry out a concrete assignment that demands fulfillment. Therein, he or she cannot be replaced, nor can his/her life be repeated; thus everyone's task is unique as is his/her specific opportunity."

The most widely known existential psychologist in America is Rollo May. He was born in Ada, Ohio in 1909 and lived until 1994. His ideas are different from the mainstream European theorists inasmuch as his were greatly influenced by American humanism and pragmatism. He also had the ability to tie together existentialism with other therapeutic approaches such as those of Freud or Jung. He was unique, but an existentialist through and through. Some of his quotes are:

"The opposite of courage in our society is not cowardice, it is conformity."

"If you do not express your own original ideas, if you do not listen to your own being, then you will have betrayed yourself."

Even before the advent of Rollo May, existentialism was slowly being introduced into the United States in the 1920's and 1930's, mostly in university classrooms. In 1959 Psychologists Rollo May, Abraham Maslow and Herman Feifel took part in the American Psychological Association's Symposium about Existential Psychology and Therapy. This led to existentialism becoming a "buzz" word of psychology during the 1960's. It became a significant theoretical approach to modern psychology as well as a major system of psychotherapy. It derived in part from a general awareness and anxiety about existence that resulted from World War II and the Korean War.

May's enormously popular book, "Love And Will" was on the U.S. best-seller list for more than four months. This demonstrated that people were willing to have an open mind and question themselves and their purpose more than ever before in American history. Self-help books then began to line the shelves of bookstores as people became more open-minded to different ways of experiencing themselves as well as their existence.

Existential psychology has "come a long way baby." It is still young in its development and popularity but seems to be making a resurgence with today's youth, the author of this chapter included. I intuitively feel there is a lot more to come regarding researching the perceptions of our existence. Existential psychology's roots are strong and its message is powerful and increasingly applicable in today's society. America could certainly use a lot more existential therapists and practitioners. We have become a society of "it's not my fault" whiners. We take pills to feel like we have some meaning in our lives rather than creating our own meaning. We blame our psychological problems on our parents or on our genes or on our schools or on our society. Instead of griping about the past or about what other people think of what we're doing, we need to realize the shortness of our lives on earth and be aware of the powerful decisions that we can take—each and every day. Only then will begin to seize the day!

LeAnn Gentry is a promising 22 year old from Le Claire, Iowa. She is a highly intelligent, loyal, considerate and empathic young woman and is hereby encouraged to pursue a career in "existential psychotherapy." She is currently employed as a "First Mate" on a Mississippi Riverboat and simultaneously works at The Davenport Country Club, which searching for the perfect "existential" college or university.

4. Existentialism And Education

by Mary T. Haaf and Austin C. Wedemeyer

'I Think, Therefore I Am'

Human intelligence and emotional feeling set us apart from the rest of the animal kingdom. The highest form of education is the creation of an environment in which the developing human organism is immersed in learning opportunities, supported and encouraged by parents, teachers and the community at large to feed the voracious appetites of the human intellect to learn, grow and develop; to foster a lifelong joy of learning.

Human infants show the ability to learn and to respond to their environment at a very early stage of development. They respond to sounds, pressures and temperature changes even in the womb and the mood and emotions of the mother are often experienced by the developing human organism. This is the beginning of a life-long learning adventure.

Humans have an innate appetite for learning and the unique ability to learn and express language is one of the best examples of our complex learning ability. The challenge to the community is to release the constraints to learning and assist the student to develop a creativity and openness to new ideas, emotions and feelings. Nevertheless, we must resist the temptation to guide, direct and in some cases dominate the student but rather support and assist the student in his never-ending quest for knowledge, feeling and understanding.

The challenge to the education community which includes parents, teachers and others in the community is to provide a rich and rewarding environment; testing, encouraging and satisfying both intellect and emotional feeling; fostering innate creativity, understanding, emotions, and thus enhancing the learning of complex problem solving.

We must avoid the desire to impart our ideas and biases to the student for this would mean hampering and inhibiting the unfettered search for knowledge which is the right and destiny of every individual. This is the subtle challenge of education in the existentialist tradition; treading that fine line between providing a rich learning environment while avoiding the almost overwhelming desire to provide 'what is best for the student.' Rather, we must provide assistance and encourage the student's search for his own identity and learn to feel as an "authenticated individual." Expose and empower the student to ever more complex and challenging ideas, problems and feelings but avoid the desire to impose, direct or restrict the growth and direction the student chooses.

We have all seen young students frustrated by the constraints of the educational system whether by parental rules, school curricula or societal conventions, thereby inhibiting the ability or desire of the student to learn a particular subject, whether it be dinosaurs or space travel, games or role-playing, when the student shows that readiness to learn.

However, we must foster and encourage the student to master the tools which facilitate learning and open avenues to explore, enlighten and enhance understanding and problem solving. At every stage the student must be encouraged to take personal responsibility for his/her education and accomplishments, to strive to reach his/her potential, to reach that stage where the teacher feels that mixture of pleasure and anxiety when the student demonstrates the ability to achieve greater insight, understanding and passion than the teacher is capable of providing.

Observation, testing, and assessment may reveal latent talents or special interests of the student. Such newly discovered interests or talents can suggest to the teacher more specialized or unique areas of study that the student might not currently be aware of and thus provide a wider scope of educational opportunities for the student to explore. Literature rich in cultural ideas or diverse thought and opinion may encourage the student to explore an ever wider range of subjects from which the student could then choose his favorites or seek to challenge his own strengths and weaknesses. Recognition that a student may be more adept and skillful than his or her own professor in a particular (or many) subject matters, is perhaps the greatest gift an "existential" teacher can give to his/her student.

When the student achieves that new level of understanding it is time to forge a new path and to stake out the intellectual territory that is uniquely his own; to question conventional wisdom, to develop new philosophies, insights and understanding, perhaps to pen new novels, poems and dramas. That is the goal of the existentialist educational tradition, to launch a new genius upon the world, full of passion and ideas, emotions and feelings that stimulate and excite the rest of humanity. And almost inevitably, this new, 'renaissance mind' will want to transmit this appetite for life-long joy of learning to a new generation. Thus the existentialist education tradition can be self-fulfilling and sustaining because it engenders a desire to pass this insight and understanding on to a new generation. The student reared in the existentialist tradition becomes the teacher of the new generation.

The vivacious and multi-talented Mary Haaf possesses a BS degree from The University of Iowa, majoring in Elementary Education (K-9), with minors in music and social studies. She obtained a Masters degree in Education and Leadership from Xavier University in Chicago, Illinois. Like so many of the contributors to this work, Mary serves in a variety of roles, including but in no way limited to: educator (34 years at the Muscatine, Iowa School District), drama coach, director, actor, curriculum designer and presenter. Mary is a loving and devoted spouse, mother and grandmother.

Austin C. Wedemeyer was born into an Iowa farm family in 1938. He briefly attended Loras College and graduated from the U.S. Air Force Academy in 1962. He completed his flight training in 1963 and flew B-52s for more than 20 years. He served in the Air Force for a total of 27 years, such service including assignments in Vietnam, France and Belgium. He completed a Master of Education at the University of Arizona, Tucson, AZ (1971) and an MBA at Auburn University, Montgomery AL (1975). He taught French to Cadets at the Air Force Academy, served as the Air Force Advisor to the Naval War College, Newport, RI and taught ROTC at the University of California, Berkeley, CA. Upon retirement from the Air Force in 1989, Austin became an airline pilot, flying with American Eagle Airlines and Northwest Airlines. He retired from the Airlines in Feb. 2007. He currently manages several rental properties and raises Kiwi fruit in Suisun Valley, California.

5. Programmed Performance Enhancing Drug Use In Sport: Cheating the Spontaneous Spirit of Competition

by Dr. Gary Gaffney

As a youth growing up in Algiers, Albert Camus played soccer (football) passionately and joyfully. Camus was quoted on the value of his sporting experience: "After many years during which I saw many things, what I know most surely about morality and the duty of man, I owe to sport and learned it on the Racing Universitaire Algerios (football team)."

Camus was said to have learned teamwork, loyalty, and a sense of fairness on the athletic field. Although tuberculosis shortened Camus' athletic career, sport clearly affected his existential leanings. When he wrote about the complex and convoluted morality of political and religious establishments, it is said he often longed for the more simple morality such as that which he found on the soccer field.

Wouldn't Camus be surprised to read the sports pages in 2008? The 'live-in-the-moment' milieu of a game, the clear moral choice of the home team heroes over the evil visitors, and the simple declaration of a winner, appear to be replaced by the convoluted protocols for 'performance-enhancing drug' tests, the arguments over asterisked athletic marks, and the remanded track records following drug-cheating scandals. A winner is not a winner anymore. A winner must be vetted through a series of intrusive urine drug tests and tedious court challenges.

The exultation of the moment for the Tour de France winner in 2007—Floyd Landis—was replaced with years of legal proceedings when an excess of the male hormone testosterone turned up in the Landis' post-race urine testing. The 2008 Tour de France ended before Landis was ruled a dope-cheat, then stripped of his 2007 Tour title. 'Live-in-the-moment' indeed; as of March 2008, Landis' status as the 2007 Tour de France winner continues in limbo awaiting one more international sports court appeal. A series of legal battles and arbitration boards irreconcilably replaced the triumph of victory at the finish line.

When was the existential joy of sporting competition replaced by the forensic exercise of anti-doping testing protocols and laboratory probes into the hormonal status of athletes? As systematic training and preparation for competition employed pharmacological enhancement of physiological processes to produce super-athletes, pre- programmed for victory, the spontaneous exultation of clean, fair, and exhilarating competition degenerated into calculated contrived 'scientifically' determined winners. These programmed winners not only enjoyed the adulation awarded to athletic achievement, they harvested the financial and political spoils of their tainted victories. The path to a gold medal became akin to an amoral business plan, utilizing a highly structured training schedule augmented with a pharmaceutical doping scheme that would tip the scales of competition in favor of the artificially and illegally enhanced athlete. The path to a huge professional signing bonus and a large salary went through covert drug enhancement combined with bombastic (can training be characterized in this way?) physical training.

A Brief History of Olympic Doping

The Olympic Games were reinstituted in 1896 to promote world harmony by bringing international youth together in an environment of intense but fair competition. As nation-building and national chauvinism developed in political post-World War I Europe, Hitler's regime attempted to use the 1936 Berlin Olympics to make a statement about the Aryan Superman. The stage became set for national movements to manipulate sport for political motives.

Doping—the use of performance enhancing drugs (PEDs) appeared almost as soon as the modern Olympic Games sprung up in Europe. In the 1904 Olympic Games, Thomas J. Hicks, was given strychnine and brandy by his coach apparently during a race. Decades later, Canada's Ben Johnson stunned the world when he cheated to win a drug-enhanced 100 meter dash in 1988.

Although the Nazi regime of Adolph Hitler is often cited as the first systematic political program to use drug enhanced athletes as political-sports supermen, it was the subsequent German Democratic Republic that designed a comprehensive doping machine to produce artificially-enhanced athletes dominating world sporting competition. The GDR perfected the cheating culture to advance their political goals and international prestige.

Considering the prominence of the Olympics on a world stage, and the huge public relations benefit of an Olympic victory bestowed on the athlete and his or her country, it was predictable that an immoral athlete and a conniving political regime would develop systematic training and doping programs to manipulate the spontaneous joy of Olympic competition.

Ben Johnson, World Class Olympic Drug-Cheat

On an individual basis, the Canadian sprinter Ben Johnson utilized the most infamous individual systematic approach of training and doping to overwhelm his competition in the Olympic sprints. In the 1980's Johnson was a competitive sprinter, but generally inferior to his American rival Carl Lewis. Johnson's coach and his physician sought out the latest of PEDs to bulk-up Johnson with slabs of thick muscle for power, and to decrease the amount of fat tissue on the sprinter for explosiveness. Combined with brutal training, the PEDs Johnson utilized increased his speed and power. Thus an extremely muscular Johnson—with jaundiced sclera due to anabolic steroids —began defeating the American sprinter Lewis in international competition prior to the 1988 Games.

Johnson's systematic drug-cheating culminated in the sprinter winning a convincing victory in the most glamorous race of the 1988 Olympics Games—the 100 meter dash. Johnson's powerful strides blasted him past Lewis and to the finish line ahead of an impressive field of world-class sprinters in Seoul Korea in 1988; only later was it learned that the majority of the runners in the race also used PEDs to increase their speed. Thus it appears Johnson employed the best pharmacist of the field.

Johnson brandished his victory particularly brazenly over his American rival Lewis at the finish line. First viewed as an existential moment of exhilaration when the Canadian sprinter vanquished the well known American sprinter, Johnson's moment turned sinister when he tested positive for the anabolic steroid stanozol (Winstrol). In a bizarre paradox the Canadian's moment of victory was quickly changed to a moment of humiliation when Johnson was stripped of the gold medal.

Johnson strenuously objected to the doping finding. At first he denied that he used PEDs. However, it became clear his body was toxic with an anabolic steroid. Later Johnson claimed sabotage affected the positive dope test, which was also rejected by authorities (although Johnson's physician might have injected Johnson with a traceable steroid in retaliation for an insult).

Johnson's dishonor resulted in the Dublin Commission being formed to investigate PED use in Canadian sport. Evidence indicated Johnson used a multitude of PEDs including anabolic steroids and human growth hormone (HGH). His coach and his physician conspired to promote the illegal PED use. Johnson's former lawyer, Richard Pound later became head of the World Anti-Doping Agency (WADA) where he attacked doping with a vengeance.

Despite denial and alibis for the Olympic doping Ben Johnson's urine again tested positive for an anabolic steroid later in his career proving the sprinter grew dependant upon artificial enhancement to compete in races. For his misadventures Johnson—once the most celebrated Canadian athlete in history —now rates as one of the most despised Canadians in history. The athlete who gave Canadians an exulted moment of pure celebration now rests in Canadian infamy.

Even before Ben Johnson's ignoble 1988 downfall due to anabolic steroids, the world's most heinous systematic doping program churned along east of the Rhine River—The East German doping machine.

The East German Doping Machine

As the Olympic Games became more and more politically charged in the cold war environs of the 1950's, countries on both sides of the Iron Curtain developed plans to promote their political systems through Olympic Games recognition. None showed a more ruthless, organized and regimented system than the German Democratic Republic (the GDR, the official name of East Germany). Relatively obscure, impoverished, and lackluster, the GDR and its leaders hungered for international recognition.

Over 10 volumes of government documents laid out the GDR doping system. The central plan called the 'State Planning Theme 14.25' purported to enhance the prestige and standing of the GDR through international and Olympic competition. A chillingly detailed and meticulously designed protocol snatched promising young athletes from their parental homes to train at the SC Dynamo in Berlin. Young athletes, including teenage females were dosed with anabolic steroids, as well as other PEDs. The sinister plan completely controlled the young athletes' work-outs, schooling, social encounters, drug regimens, and family visitations. Because the girls' libidos increased with the hormones, birth control pills became part of the schedule.

Far from the spontaneous joy of sport, the GDR plan answered to the highest levels of the GDR: President Erich Honecker, and GDR Olympic Czar Manfred Ewald, and the head of government sports medicine Manfred Hoppner. The doping machine continued over decades, enforced by the GDR secret police STASI—linked to the Third Reich secret police.

GDR doctors, coaches, and trainers documented athletic performances to study drug doses and combinations thereof, which produced successful performances. The GDR enlisted an East German pharmaceutical company—Jenapharm—to develop and manufacture anabolic steroids. The GDR built a world class anti-doping testing lab at Kreischa which enabled the GDR athletes to beat anti-doping testing in international competitions.

The results of the East German Doping machine produced unparalleled athletic achievement for a country with such a small population. The doping continued for decades, with a crowning achievement at the 1980 Montreal Olympics where the East German women's swimming team won 11 of 13 gold medals. East German women continue to hold world records that have never been approached by any other athletes since the GDR hormonal freaks dominated track and field as well.

The GDR doping machine came unhinged when the Berlin Wall fell and the Iron Curtain dissolved. Courageous doctors and bold former athletes risked their lives to reveal this story (The STASI continued to be an underground element of German society). However, the former GDR athletes continue to suffer physical and psychological side effects due to the systematic use of dangerous PEDs. One world class shot putter Heidi Krieger is now Hans Krieger, following a life-long emotional instability at least in part attributed to the anabolic steroid use of the GDR program. Health problems also appear to include an excess of birth defects in the children of the doped swimmers.

Thus, in the sporting arena, where existential joy should be experienced in its purest form, the entire world has witnessed a massive fraud constructed around the systematic undermining of spontaneous athletic competition.

Although the East German doping machine has ground to a halt, the grandiose plans of the designers inspired another doping machine, only this one centered in the American shining city by the bay—San Francisco. The reverberations of the Bay Area Lab Cooperative (BALCO) continue to be felt today.

BALCO: America's Systematic Doping Machine.

Late in 1995 a mustachioed man carrying a black bag began appearing at international track events. The man—Victor Conte—owned a small San Francisco supplement company which featured a Zinc-Magnesium-Aluminum product for athletic enhancement. With relatively modest beginnings, this former musician (Bass of the Tower of Power) would pervert American track and field, professional football, major league baseball, and the cult activity of body building.

Conte built an enterprise in the Bay Area starting with track and field stars. BALCO first initiated a program denominated: 'Operation World Record'. With a systematic doping program incredibly similar to the East German doping machine, BALCO doped elite world class athletes with state of the art pharmaceutics, measured their hormonal responses in labs, and kept meticulous records to measure intervention outcomes.

Conte focused on track and field where his charges included 100 M world record holder Tim Montgomery, Olympic gold medalist Marion Jones, shot-putter CJ Hunter, and UK sprinter Dwain Chambers. BALCO sought out a chemist from Illinois who synthesized unknown anabolic steroids to pass anti-doping tests. The combine gave illicit drugs like testosterone, HGH, modafinil, Clomid, and others to world class athletes thus enhancing their performance.

At the peak of the BALCO operation, the firm distributed PEDs to prominent MLB players including Barry Bonds, Gary Sheffield, and Jason Giambi. BALCO supplied NFL players including Bill Romanovsky and Dana Stubblefield steroids and HGH. BALCO PEDs directly affected the most visible sporting records in the world—the single season and career home run marks. Barry Bonds faces perjury charges in 2008 for alleged false testimony in the BALCO trials. Bonds—previously a sure-fire Baseball Hall of Fame member—may never see the inside of Cooperstown, except as a spectator.

The pervasiveness of PEDs, designed to steal honest sporting competition for drug-cheats, appears to be pervasive. Baseball's Mitchell Report released in 2007 documented the influence of these drugs on an American institution; the greatest pitcher since Cy Young—Roger Clemens—finds himself currently being investigated by 3 governmental agencies for perjury when he testified to a Congressional inquiry on PED use in professional sports.

The Tour de France, the world's most famous cycle race has been totally corrupted by the use of blood doping, anabolic steroids, and other PEDs. The greatest cyclist to compete in the Tour—Lance Armstrong—will always remain under suspicion, although never proven to be a doper. The aforementioned Floyd Landis stands as the disgraced former winner of the 2007 Tour until he tested positive for testosterone.

Why the flood of doping in sporting events? Why the drug cheating despite harmful and sinister side-effects of the powerful hormones and other PEDs used to undermine fair competition? When did it become unpopular to rely on hard work, honest effort, and a fair level playing field to reign victorious?

Although the answers to these questions will never be simple, insight may be found with issues Albert Camus raised in critiques of modern society: There appears to be an amoral element active among drug-cheats. Although PED use violates prescription and narcotics laws, there exists an even greater violation of moral codes previously honored among sports combatants. Athletes work as hard as possible within the rules to prepare for a competition. However, using PEDs violates the rules agreed upon by athletes and administrators to keep competition fair. Thus, an athlete using banned anabolic drugs attempts to tip the balance of the game in his favor by an egregious breach of sporting morals. One may refer to the existential concept of the 'absurd' when considering the accolades, and the championships won as a consequence of this dishonorable conduct.

Modern happiness seems so fleeting that the aging athlete feels compelled to dope with testosterone keeping his hormone levels forever young. That athlete needs to stay in the public spotlight as long as possible, thus cheating younger athletes who should be establishing new careers, while draining even more money from lucrative endorsements. The aging athlete who abuses anabolic hormones to stave off the inevitable decline of abilities due to age violates the natural progression of biological processes for his monetary and narcissistic gain.

Camus railed against totalitarian governments that regimented all aspects of society. Such regimentation and absolute structural control lies behind the sport doping machines wherever they exist, be it in Germany, or in California. In this scheme, all aspects of the athlete must be controlled down to his cellular milieu and her DNA expression. The purpose of sport now becomes the financial and exploitive gain of the elite athlete (corporation, team, or country). A victory results in a huge windfall when the athlete becomes marketed to sell a commercial product, or a victory enhances the political power of the athlete's team or country. This systematic, programmed achievement lies diametrically opposed to the spontaneous exhilaration that Albert Camus experienced in competition and about which he wrote in his novels and essays.

Can sport ever return to the existential and spontaneous exhilaration of a simple athletic competition, where gifted athletes competing intensely but fairly gave fans a break from the regimented bureaucracy seemingly in control of every other aspect of life? With the infiltration of doping and PEDs—and potentially genetic performance enhancement—it appears that a return to the true Olympic spirit of sport will be very difficult task indeed.

Dr. Gary Gaffney is a gifted Child Psychiatrist affiliated with The University of Iowa Hospitals and Clinics in Iowa City. He has, throughout the course of his career, integrated principles of "existential humanism" into his psychiatric practice as well as his personal life.

Gaffney manages a blog entitled: The "Steroid Nation" in which he promotes discussion regarding the use of performance and appearance enhancing drugs and the impact of same on the sporting establishment, the popular culture and on all of our lives. Gaffney has been married to Marcia Gaffney, a Registered Nurse, for 30 years and is the proud father of three children. He resides in Solon, Iowa and is an avid sports fan as well as an overall "great guy."

6. Physical Perfections or Physique Perversions? Appearance Enhancing Drugs, Procedures, and the Natural Life

by Dr. Gary Gaffney

Sylvester Stallone, star of the 'Rocky' and 'Rambo' series of movies, despite his age of 60, continues to portray movie action heroes on the big screen. One would expect that a cinematic action hero would be a younger actor, exhibiting overly-developed skeletal muscles combined with a trim narrow waist. Rigorous exercise, a healthy diet, and clean living in a relatively young man should produce such an action movie idol. Yet, Stallone—at an age many men consider to be retirement age—displays an incredibly ripped physique, the envy of males of any age. In the 2007 movie 'Rocky Balboa', Stallone appeared leaner and meaner than he did three decades earlier for 'Rocky'. What combination of genes, diet, and workouts produced this god, springing from a modern fountain of youth? Or should the question be "which professionals engineered the actor's enhanced physical appearance?"

Between the release of Rocky in December 2006, and the filming of the latest Rambo installment, Stallone's traveling party landed in Sydney Australia carrying an interesting supply of pharmaceutics. The Australian customs police discovered cases of synthetic human growth hormone (HGH) and injectable anabolic androgenic steroids (AAS). The fountain of youth Stallone discovered springs forth from the cornucopia of pharmaceutical hormones now produced by the drug industry. Although the actor believes in his hormonal artificial youth, Stallone's anabolic drug regimen is dangerous to his health. HGH and AASs affect the heart, liver, kidneys, prostate, testicles, and tendons in ways Stallone does not yet—or never will —comprehend.

The Cult of Artificial Appearance Enhancement

Medical doctors prescribe HGH and AAS for legitimate medical diseases including childhood growth failure, severe catabolic states produced by burns, and the muscle wasting caused by Autoimmune Deficiency Syndrome (AIDS). However, bodybuilders and athletes diverted so many anabolic drugs from legitimate uses that in 1991, the US Congress moved anabolic steroids to a very tightly controlled and regulated drug class called 'Schedule III'. HGH is not a scheduled controlled drug; however it is treated that way by federal narcotics agents.

The early abusers of HGH and AAS consisted of the narcissistic bodybuilding culture congregating in sunny Southern California, the iron-moving power lifters in gym towns like York PA, and renegade Olympic athletes working with unethical physicians and trainers seeking an edge in athletic competition. Later HGH and AAS use spread to major league baseball players, NFL football athletes, and cult niche entertainers such as pro wrestling personalities. At some point in the 21st century, the use of these powerful hormones by non-athletes seeking to simply enhance the appearance of their bodies overtook the athletes using the drugs to gain an edge in competition. In fact, a new syndrome needed to be coined to describe these male narcissistic chameleons: Body Dysmorphic Syndrome, also known as the Adonis Syndrome when seen in bodybuilding males and females.

In a companion chapter, there was a discussion concerning the infiltration of athletic events by programs of systematic drug doping. This development parallels the hijacking of the arts, entertainment, and even the evening news, by the culture of enhanced physique and the expression of contrived beauty. It would be difficult to view a movie, a television show, a Broadway play, or even a legitimate news broadcast without seeing a male or female who underwent cosmetic surgery, or body augmentation, or Botox injections, or the enhancement of physique from the hormonal drugs of youth. The cultural and performing arts now present paradoxically grossly beautiful faces and bodies and as a monument to artificial 'Appearance Enhancement'. The drugs used to enhance physical appearance are known as 'Appearance Enhancing Drugs' (AEDs) similar to the athletic Performance Enhancing Drugs (PEDs).

What becomes projected on the large screen of film and the small screen of TV becomes the idol for Main Street. Anabolic steroids became routine in gyms across the world; steroid abuse now constitutes a major drug problem in drug treatment programs in the United Kingdom and in the United States. Interesting that often the criminal element distributing the illegal drugs will be pursued by law enforcement agents who themselves manifest significant problems in the use of illegal PEDs and AEDs. Cases of capital crimes involving juiced policemen now make their way through the court systems where the existence of 'roid' rage—hormonal drug rages—complicate crime prosecutions.

Recent studies and books document the use of AEDs and PEDs in college and high school cheerleaders, young prostitutes in Indian brothels, gay men cruising the bar scene, and legions of men and women trying to appear youthful, muscular, and lean.

The development of cosmetic surgery and artificial body parts took similar routes. Developed to help patients recover from burns, surgery, and other medical problems, these bio-medical devices and surgical procedures oftentimes appear to be diverted for superficial cosmetic purposes. Americans now spend over 10 billion dollars per year for cosmetic surgery of not only stars on the screen, but also non-actors, simply wishing to enhance their appearance.

Baseball legend Roger Clemens recently denied the use of PEDs in a congressional hearing; however he did admit that his wife Debbie used HGH prior to a rather bizarre revealing photo shoot in <u>Sports Illustrated</u>. A 39 year-old mother of four, enhanced by breast augmentation and injections of HGH, Debbie Clemens poses in a revealing bikini with her Hall of Fame husband's last name inscribed on her bikini top. For what reason? To impress the masses of sports fans that not only is the great Roger Clemens a baseball stud nonpareil, but that his gorgeous wife and mother of four children maintains rock hard abdominal muscles combined with the large breasts of a Barbie doll? Is there any better example of the anti-existential images of systematic and planned narcissism, worshiped by millions as icons of modern culture?

Chris Benoit and the homi-suicide that shook the sports-entertainment world

For decades the entertainment called 'pro wrestling' existed in a fantasy world of staged matches that generally exploited an audience's blood lust, pent-up aggression, and black and white morality of good versus evil, e.g. Handsome Harley Race and Pretty Boy Larry Hennig versus Dick the Bruiser and the Crusher.

In the 80's, an east coast wrestling promoter named Vince McMahon changed pro wrestling from a violent, weekend beer fest, to a 'sports entertainment' venue replete with exaggerated story lines featuring super heroes with steroid-enhanced physiques. As the success of the WWE (World Wrestling Entertainment) and progenitors exploded, the story lines became more bizarre as the wrestlers attained even greater physical girth and enhanced public stature. Superstar Hulk Hogan captured the attention of a nation of crazed fans arguing whether or not pro wrestling was fake.

Despite steroid trafficking charges in the 1990's, McMahon's empire grew. Paralleling the trends in culture, politics, and even legitimate sport, pro wrestling continued forward in a world of pre-programmed scenarios, steroid-enhanced physiques, and a grinding schedule of more and more bizarre features for pay-for-view TV. A warning shot came when a female wrestling star—Ms. Elizabeth—was found dead of an overdose in her pro wrestling boyfriend—Lex Lugar's—house. The real Elizabeth Hulette hung around pro wrestling for years, flashing a surgical bust, and a redone face. Live-in boyfriend Lawrence Pfohl used AAS to pack on superhero muscle to his former Penn State linebacker frame.

Hulette's blood contained alprazolam (Xanax), hydrocodone (a narcotic), and vodka. Her live-in boyfriend Lawrence Pfohl surrendered a cache of oxycotin, anabolic steroids, testosterone, HGH, and alprazolam. The bizarre anti-existential world of pro wrestling turned even more sinister as the male muscles ballooned and the female bust lines boomed.

Apparently paying no heed to the warning shots fired in the Atlanta home of Hulette and Pfohl, the WWE continued marketing a mix of programmed artificial sex and violence. In June of 2007, the absurd world of fantasy, supported by illicit drugs and enhanced cosmetics imploded into violence. A pro wrestler named Chris Benoit succumbed to multifarious demons as he strangled his 45 year-old wife on Friday, June 22; one day later he drugged and suffocated his 7 year-old son Daniel. On Sunday Benoit hung himself in his home gym.

Toxicology analysis of Nancy Benoit's body showed hydrocodone, hydromorphine, Xanax, and alcohol in her blood. Chris Benoit's body contained high doses of testosterone, hydrocodone, and Xanax. Speculation also centered on chronic brain injuries Benoit suffered from the rigors of pro wrestling. There was no spectacular, fictional story line to save the destruction of this family; the calculated use of narcotics, anabolic steroids, and chronic fake entertainment-sports injuries doomed the life of a young family. The absurd in this case was all too real.

Anna Nicole Smith

Another counterpoint to the existential spontaneity and genuineness of life can be witnessed in the sordid life of Anna Nicole Smith and her motley crew. Smith rose to 'stardom' based on breast implants, dyed hair, liposuction, plastic surgery, and regular injections of AEDs. Smith fabricated her own celebrity by marrying a rich elderly man from Texas, then engaging in a series of misadventures, demonstrating that notoriety requires no particular talent other than the exposition of large augmented breasts. Smith's life and death bestowed physical and emotional carnage upon almost everyone who came into contact with her.

Smith died in Florida, with an incredible cocktail of prescription and illicit drugs found in her system: the sedative chloral hydrate; 4 benzodiazepines: Klonopin (clonazepam), Ativan (lorazepam), Serax (oxazepam), and Valium (diazepam); Benadryl (diphenhydramine) ; and Topamax an anti-convulsant drug. Smith also used B-12, immunoglobins, and HGH, likely for the purported anti-aging properties of the drugs. The forensic pathologist attributed Smith's death to the mix of sedatives she ingested. Although use of HGH can cause serious side effects including cardiac hypertrophy, the only mention of HGH referred to injections causing abscesses in Smith's gluteus muscles.

From small town, low-level exotic dancer, Anna Nicole Smith's rise to infamy, and fall to an intoxicated stuperous demise can be seen as another gross example of the culture of artificial narcissism. Diametrically opposed to a life of spontaneity and meaning through action, thought and achievement, Smith's actions appear premeditated to draw maximum media attention based on minimum real achievement. Has anyone in the history of the world become more known for becoming a completely artificial construction of celebrity than Anna Nicole Smith?

Appearance Enhancement

Bodybuilders and movie starlets lead the parade of artificial appearance enhancement: Bloated muscles, and ageless faces. However, appearance enhancement now trickles down to all segments of society, and all socio-economic levels. Cheerleaders in high school and college take anabolic steroids for strength. Prostitutes in India are given anabolic steroids to hasten puberty in young girls to expand the stable of available working females. Gay and straight men take steroids and HGH to trim down their bodies while enhancing their muscular development, for sexual attractiveness. Rap stars ordered steroids and HGH through Florida Internet pharmacies, apparently to achieve a hardened and muscular street look. Actors such as Stallone use testosterone and HGH to enable them to continue to play the roles of matinee hunks even as they age well past their natural prime. Botox and plastic surgery pervade television and movie personalities; can anyone actually smile on the evening news anymore?

Why the race to unnatural plastic and artificial appearances? Why must every personality sport almost identical cookie-cutter lean muscular physiques, thin noses, and injected puffy lips?

The technology of artificial enhancement appears to have raced past the social discussion of the ethics of chemical and physical biological engineering. Medical science can enhance almost every human through hormonal, material, and surgical methods. This enhancement goes beyond the traditional medical role of treating disease. The enhancement of normal or gifted humans with interventions originally designed to treat disease is a new and relatively unanalyzed frontier.

Has there ever been a serious discussion of the limits of enhancement? At what stage does a human being become some sort of cyborg operating as a combination of pharmaceutical freak and surgically reconstructed android. When might it be considered unethical to meddle with a human who does not suffer from a disease—one who simply wishes to pharmaceutically enhance a biological parameter for an advantage in beauty competition, or to attract prime movie roles, or procure sexual partners, all the while generating profits from their booty?

As human idols try to extend their images beyond what nature (or genetics) dealt them, anxiety appears to follow— these enhancements are not without psychological side effects or medical consequences. In each example referred to in this chapter, the AEDs and the plastic surgery were accompanied with narcotics and benzodiazepines apparently for pain or relaxation. The pursuit of becoming the matinee god, or the superhero wrestler, or the captivating goddess also leads to paranoia and anxiety about the future. A career built on superficial external beauty or perfection would be self-limiting; thus the 'public personality' must increase the dose, or pour on the Botox, or submit to even more plastic surgery to stay ahead of the competition. An artificial enhancement nuclear arms race ensues to stay abreast of competitors.

This programmed pursuit of happiness or fame or idolatry stands in diametric opposition to the existential pursuit of the spontaneous life. Rather than accept and embrace the effects of maturity or imperfection, or aging, current idols fight nature, and apparently suffer when the inevitable deleterious side-effects occur—the steroids are less effective or lead to heart or liver damage, the surgery leads to bizarre facial mutilation, or the side effects of the drugs lead to disability, depression and death. Two of the more notorious of these stories were related in the material here; however rest assured that although these case studies of Benoit and Smith present spectacularly haunting contemporary stories, other similar stories occur on a frequent basis when the artificial enhancement overwhelms biological compensatory mechanisms.

It might be argued that the science and technology race into the artificial world of cyborg humans, artificially enhanced actors, and Botoxed weathermen and women is but a manifestation of a larger struggle—the struggle of ethicists to define what the roles of these scientific advances should be in humans. Is it psychologically healthy to idolize an actress who utilized plastic surgery to correct her nose, Botox to smooth her wrinkles, silicon to enhance her bust, HGH to reduce her waistline, and implants to round out her buttocks? Should we be concerned that she needs Adderall to concentrate in the morning, Zoloft to treat feelings of emptiness, Xanax to reduce anxiety, Lasix to reduce water weight, a birth control pill to regulate menstruation, Vicodin to reduce the pain from surgery, and Lunesta to fall asleep at night?

It may be that AEDs, plastic surgery, implants and the other current artificial enhancements are simply the first volley in the battle between natural biological man, and artificial enhanced and engineered man. This is a battle carried out with stem-cell research, fought in the laboratory to produce fetuses for infertile couples, and waged in the Ivy League classroom as over-achieving students compete, each on stimulant medicines to increase their concentration. This is a battle for survival that features not only natural biological factors—genetics, mentoring, work, and motivation—but also designed or artificial factors —drug injections, implanted devices, and engineered materials —into the biological struggle of the fittest.

Is this a struggle we want in society? Isn't it time for a dialog to begin between the ethicists and the salespeople? Doesn't an existential view that promotes a natural life and an unenhanced biology deserve a hearing? Shouldn't there be a dialog between those who appreciate the way humans age naturally and those who would prolong youth at any cost?

If this dialogue does not begin soon, the science and the technology of AEDs—the pills, the injectable biologicals and altered genes as well as substitute anatomical parts—will race past the point when ethicists, philosophers and moral leaders can sound warnings that our heroes are chemical creations and our goddesses are silicon divas. These enhanced cyborgs will be leading society down a programmed path that contains sinister dangers, both known and unknown—the antithesis of the spontaneous, playful path of an existential 'live in the moment' world. False idols indeed.

Dr. Gary Gaffney's short biographical sketch is set forth at the end of the previous chapter, which he also wrote.

7. Existentialism And Judicial Realism

by Richard V. Campagna

Although I requested a couple of other legal practitioners to write this chapter for our book, time and circumstances did not permit such. That being said, I am very pleased to "do it myself" because I am such a firm believer in the legal theory/philosophy which I am about to describe.

A great deal does not have to be said to make the requisite points. And I must credit Wikipedia, the free encyclopedia, whose brief article on this theme entitled "Legal Realism" was so helpful to me and should be extremely helpful to all readers. So here goes:

Legal (or Judicial) Realism is a family of theories about the true and essential nature of the law, developed in the first half of the 20th century in the United States (American Legal Realism). There was also a parallel movement taking place in Scandinavia. The essential tenet of legal realism is that all law, whether it derived from the common law or civil law tradition, is made by human beings, interpreted by human beings, executed by human beings, and as a consequence thereof, is subject to human foibles, frailties, imperfections and existential arbitrariness and subjectivity.

Justice Oliver Wendell Holmes is considered by many to be the driving force behind American Legal Realism (other influences include Roscoe Pound, Benjamin Cardozo and Wesley Hohfeld). Wikipedia informs us that the chief inspiration for Scandinavian Legal Realism derives from the works of Axel Hagerstrom.

Other well known representatives of American Legal/ Judicial Realism were: Karl Llewellyn, formulator of the Uniform Commercial Code (which is said to have been created with Legal Realism as its underlying philosophy), Felix S. Cohen, Arthur Linton Corbin, Jerome Frank (my personal favorite), Robert Lee Hale, Herman Oliphant, Thurman Arnold, Hessel Untema, Max Radin, William Underhill Moore, Leon Green and Fred Rodell. Wikipedia further advises that the most famous representatives of Scandinavian Legal Realism were: Alf Ross, Karl Olivecrona and A.Vilhelm Lundstedt.

Karl Llewellyn was a major figure in the debate and teaching of legal realism while a professor at Columbia Law School. As in Christianity, Buddhism, Islam, Existentialism or any similar movement, no single set of beliefs are shared by all legal realists, but many of the realists share one or more of the following ideas:

➤ Belief in the indeterminacy of law. Many of the so-called "founders" of legal realism believed that the laws on the books (statutes, case law, administrative determinations, rules and regulations, etc.) did not determine the results of legal disputes, for the most part. Jerome Frank, whose version of legal/judicial realism I was taught in my law school jurisprudence and contracts courses, is famously credited with the notion that a judicial decision might well be determined by what the judge had for breakfast, whether he or she got up on the wrong side of the bed as well as by the trier of the fact's personal philosophy, religious beliefs and socio-economic status.

☛ Belief in the importance of interdisciplinary approaches to law. Many of the realists were and continue to be interested in sociological and anthropological approaches to the study of law, myself clearly included in this group. Karl Llewellyn's book "The Cheyenne Way" is a famous example of this tendency.

☛ Belief in 'legal instrumentalism,' the view that the law should be used as a tool to achieve social purposes and to balance competing societal interests. With respect to this last concept, it is apparent to me that a "judicially realistic" analysis of the law suggests that legal instrumentalism is clearly being practiced today. That does not mean that I like it, or believe it should be...but quite frankly, there is no other way in man-made systems such as ours.

The so-called heyday of the legal/judicial realism movement in America commenced in the 1920's and lasted through the early 1940's. Following the end of World War II, as its leading figures retired or became less active, legal realism gradually started to fade as a theme that was taught to lawyers and legal practitioners. That being said, such did not signify that as a legal/analytical/theoretical tool for analyzing legal decisions, "legal realism" went away. Just like "existential philosophy" according to most existential philosophers, myself included, this analysis of the human condition does not ever go away. It represents the only reasonable, pragmatic and non-absurd approach to understanding reality throughout the ages.

Despite its decline in mass popularity and coverage in the popular culture, realists continue to influence a wide spectrum of jurisprudential schools today, including but not limited to critical legal studies (whose major proponents include Duncan Kennedy and Roberto Unger), feminist legal theory, critical race theory and law and economics (scholars such as Richard Posner and Richard Epstein at The University of Chicago). In addition, Wikipedia advises that legal realism eventually led to the recognition of disciplines such as political science and studies of judicial behavior as specialized disciplines within the social sciences.

Legal Realism emerged as an anti-formalist and empirically oriented response to the legal formalism of Dean Christopher Columbus Langdell and the American Law Institute (ALI) as well as to the "legal positivism" of Europe and Latin America and the "mechanical jurisprudence" or "science of law," with which both Langdell and the ALI became associated.

In summary, legal realists, of virtually all persuasions, similar to existential philosophers, psychologists and practitioners, generally advance two claims:

1) Law is often indeterminate and that judges and other triers of fact (juries, Administrative Law Judges, hearing officers, arbitrators, mediators) consequently must and often do, draw upon extra-legal considerations to resolve the disputes before them

2) The best answer to the question "What is the law?" is "Whatever judges and other relevant officials do."

I can end this chapter by simply observing that our society and life in general, is best analyzed in existential/realistic terms. In virtually all of the classes that I teach and when conversing with virtually all of the people that I meet along my path, we concurrently conclude that there is an all pervasive "legal realism, journalistic realism, political realism, medical realism, psychological realism"...the list goes on and on. Realism, as described hereinabove, has become all pervasive in our society. Just spend an evening watching the analysts on The Fox News Channel to understand what I'm talking about.

All of these "realisms" are grounded in an existential philosophy which basically suggests that each and every action that each individual takes, becomes our ultimate value, because that's what we chose to do at that moment in time. Selective picking of facts and principles and application and execution of the ones we chose become our personal realities, political realities, legal realities, journalistic realities, medical and psychological realities.

It's not exactly the way we were taught these disciplines at our fancy colleges and universities and educational enrichment programs...but the foregoing sure tends to explain how things work, a lot better than the pre-packaged cultural programs, mindless, empty platitudes and governmental mandates which are inundating our lives on a daily basis.

8. Walter Jay Greenberg— Existentialist Par Excellence

by Walter Jay Greenberg

I. Soren Aabye Kierkegarrd

"...the thing is to find a truth which is true for me, to find the idea for which I can live and die"

—*Søren Aabye Kierkegaard*

Journals 1835

In what was perhaps his earliest major work *Either / Or* (1843) Kierkegaard suggests that people might effectively choose to live within either of two "existence spheres". He called these "spheres" the aesthetic and the ethical.

Aesthetical lives were lives lived in search of such things as pleasure, novelty, and romantic individualism. Kierkegaard thought that such "pleasure", such "novelty", and such "romantic individualism" would eventually tend to decay or become meaningless and this would inevitably lead to much boredom and dire frustration.

Ethical lives, meanwhile, were those being lived very much in line with a sense of duty to observe societal and confessional obligations. Such a life would be easy, in some ways, to live, yet would also involve much compromise of several genuinely human faculties and potentials. Such compromise would inevitably mean that Human integrity would tend to be eroded although lives seemed to be progressing in a bourgeois-satisfactory way.

What sort of person a person tended to become was very dependent on the life choices they made and the sort of lives they subsequently decided to lead. Neither of the "existence spheres" that Kierkegaard believed that he had identified seemed to him to offer fully satisfactory lives to Human beings.

In his later works he suggested that there was a third, religious, "sphere" wherein people accepted that they could "live in the truth" that they were "individual before the Eternal" to which they belonged. By living in this truth people could achieve a full unity of purpose with all other people who were also, individually, living in the same truth. This is the choice that he made for himself in his own efforts to live a life which he considered to be valid.

II. Jean Paul Sartre

In terms of phenomenology Jean Paul Sartre's Existentialism maintains that in man, and in man alone, existence preceded essence. This simply means that man first is, and only subsequently is this or that. In a word, man must create his own essence: it is in throwing himself into the world, suffering there, struggling there, that he gradually defines himself. This definition always remains open ended: we cannot say what this man is before he dies, or what mankind is before it has disappeared.

Sartre based his Existentialism on human free will. As individuals are free, from the moment of conception, they define their essence throughout their existence. A person's nature is what he or she has done in the past and what that person is doing at the moment. No one is complete until death, when self-definition ceases. Then, how others interpret the individual is based upon the individual's accomplishments and failings.

Existential morality arises from the fact that all choices affect others, physically and emotionally. Social responsibility results from the interdependencies of individuals. Since any living person is engaged in the process of defining self and others, ethics develop accordingly. Since the existentialist values free will and wants others to respect his or her freedom, the ethical system developed is based upon free expression.

Regarding religion, Sartre said, 'Existentialism is not atheist in the sense that it would exhaust itself in demonstrations of the non-existence of God. It declares, rather, that even if God existed that would make no difference from its point of view.'

III. Friedrich Nietzsche

Nietzsche conceived the famous phrase "God is Dead." Thus, for Nietzsche, existence emerges as a philosophical problem in his distinction between moral autonomy (as obedience to the moral law) and an autonomy "beyond good and evil." But if one is to speak of autonomy, meaning, and value at all, the mode of being beyond good and evil cannot simply be a lawless state of arbitrary and impulsive behavior. If such existence is to be thinkable there must be a standard by which success or failure can be measured. Nietzsche variously indicates such a standard in his references to "health," "strength," and "the meaning of the earth." Perhaps his most instructive indication, however, comes from aesthetics, since its concept of *style*, as elaborated in *The Gay Science*, provides a norm appropriate to the singularity of existence. To say that a work of art has style is to invoke a standard for judging it, but one that cannot be specified in the form of a general law of which the work would be a mere instance. Rather, in a curious way, the norm is internal to the work. For Nietzsche, existence falls under such an imperative of style: to create meaning and value in a world from which all transcendent supports have fallen away is to give unique shape to one's immediate inclinations, drives, and passions; to interpret, prune, and enhance according to a unifying sensibility, a ruling instinct, that brings everything into a whole that satisfies the non-conceptual, aesthetic norm of what fits, what belongs, what is appropriate.

It is interesting to note, that for all of their philosophizing, our beloved Internet implies that Kierkegaard and Sartre died religious men, and Nietzsche died insane, thinking he was Jesus.

Now for the part about Walter Jay Greenberg, existentialist.

Once you have food, shelter, and safety, you want something more. Taking it to the next step, now that you have a better quality of life for you and your family, you still want something more. This is what I think happened in the 1960's. We baby boomers, the children of the people previously mentioned (of at least a certain socio-economic level), having food, shelter, clothes, and a good education, were left asking, "Well, what is meaningful in life?" It may have started also as "What is fun in life?" We tried long hair and extreme fashions. The birth control pill brought in the free love idea. Rock music proliferated, antiwar rallies, civil rights legislation, experimentation with drugs, eastern religions. All of this was to find meaning, develop fun and frolic, satisfy natural and unnatural urges, and all of this we later had to reinterpret.

This search for meaning (in a seemingly unexplainable and perhaps meaningless cosmos), what some call existentialism, began long before that. I submit that any human, with even a spare moment to think, may try to fathom what else there might be that would be better or be more meaningful, or simply ruminating, "Why am I here?" and possibly, "Is anyone or any thing in charge? What are the rules?" This has been going on long before French, German, Danish and other philosophers wrote about it. I would place this originally with the evolution of language, allowing even early humans the luxury of pondering, wondering, bemusing their lots in life and trying to keep amused enough not to exit life.

"Walter Jay Greenberg" is what it says on my birth certificate as a correction to the original "Baby Greenberg" because my parents had not yet decided on my name. My mother said she liked "Jay" because if I got famous some day it would sound nice to say my name was "Walter Jay" and I could just drop the Greenberg. Maybe that was a WWII thing or McCarthy, I never asked.

Why did I write the piece you are now reading? Richard Campagna and I went to Brown University at the same time but did not know each other until 2007 when I joined a Brown alumni club that he founded. We have since discovered a certain connection that cannot merely be measured in trips around the sun between September 1968 and June 1972 at Brown University, in Providence Rhode Island. Something in our conversations sparked a feeling of consanguinity, and a near congruence of spirit, so Richard asked me to contribute to his book.

"What is the meaning of life? This question is far too cliché and really what does it matter?" Go see the Monty Python movie, sing, "Look on the bright side of life", and laugh at the absurdity. That question is unanswerable. So ask youself, rather, how you should conduct yourself, and feel about things, regardless of the meaning of life. This way you invent your own meaning, even if it is meaningless.

Time and space:

You have all heard someone say, "At this point in time…" English teachers will tell you that it is redundant because at this point means time, so drop the "in time" part. However, one could say, "At this point in space". I majored in Geophysics. Time and distance and how relevant mankind is, can lose significance if you are speaking cosmologically. Since Albert Einstein's famous equations, Rate x Time = Distance now has to have factored in a relativity component within which, the speed of light is a constant. My father, Herbert Greenberg, a famous mathematician once asked me: When you are on a space ship approaching the speed of light and you turn on a flash light, how fast is the light from the flash light going?" I got the answer wrong. The speed of light cannot change, so what does? The answer is time, distance, or both. You do not even have to be going at the speed of light to measure a change in time. One of the atomic clocks took a trip on a jet and the scientists measured a difference in time with the atomic clock on the ground. It was fractions of a second, but still measurable.

The Universe is expanding since the big bang, but the acceleration is not reasonable unless you put dark energy and dark matter into the equations. What are they? Einstein did not know but he provided for a "Cosmological Constant" to help sort it out. Are there more universes? A number of learned people believe such is possible. For humanity to survive the final death of this Universe when everything is so far apart that there is no interaction of atoms, the humans of that time will have had to have jumped to a different universe a lot earlier when they were able to That means they reached a level 3 civilization. Level 3 is when they have the ability to harness all the energy of this universe. (We are in level zero. 1 is when you can harness the power of the solar system; 2 you can harness all the energy of the Milky Way galaxy). By the way, since matter can neither be created nor destroyed, all of the atoms in your body, in the past, were part of different stars, nebulas, comets, and various other things before they got together to be you. Put that in your pipe and smoke it, eh.

Okay, so now where are you in space and what is happening to you? In my first Brown physics class there was discussion about Inertial Reference Frames. For example, if you are in an elevator and drop a ball, how does it look to you, compared to someone outside watching the elevator? Is North up? What is up? Actually, on earth, it is the opposite direction of the center of the Earth. Maybe maps should show Florida on top. In China, they have China at the middle of maps of the world because in Chinese, the name of the country is Middle Kingdom so it is in the middle of the world. To continue the inertial reference frame discussion, if you were somewhere in outer space and had a telescope strong enough to look at someone jumping in an elevator on earth, that person would be falling, jumping, spinning around the earth's axis, revolving around the sun, in a rotating galaxy called the Milky Way, and so forth. In addition, the person observing has to be somewhere also.

None of this negates that today you may feel good, well, bad, sick, bored, happy, or you may be asleep dreaming. So does anything matter? Personally, if I have a headache, I do not feel well or happy and then what does if matter if nothing matters, my head hurts.

This 60's and 70's dinosaur baby boomer then puts to you what to consider on how you conduct yourself:

The meaning of life, according to me, is to find meaning and happiness for yourself but not just in a self-centered way. Someone once told me that on your deathbed, no one would say with his last breath, "I should have spent more time at the office." When I blow out the candles on my birthday cake, I always wish for the same thing, happiness. This is not because I am particularly unhappy, although I can be; it is because logic dictates that if I and everyone else were happy, that would mean everything was all right—right? This right is as opposed to left —sinister (This is a linguistic and sociological joke. People thought left handed people were sinister and in schools they tried to change children to become right handed by whacking them on their dominant left hand with a ruler).

More specifically on the meaning of life, and/or how to conduct yourself, after my 57 trips around the sun, I have decided, for me, there are a number of meaningful things. First and foremost, is to care for your family members. Except for your own life, they are what is part of you and you are part of them. Be extremely careful what you do and say to your family. A family rift may never mend. Beware of this particularly. Next, be as fair as you can to everyone—The Golden Rule. You should pursue happiness, hopefully succeeding to experience moments of joy. This you need to do despite the obligations that you feel you should do for others. You have an obligation to yourself, certainly, but not to the detriment of others. It is also possible that the joy can come from trying to fulfill those needs/obligations —joy from, in fact, the caring for others. It is funny to think that Mother Theresa might condemn herself for the sin of pride of enjoying caring for others. Now the L word, love has to do with the joy you derive being involved with someone else and this can give you bliss. You can also love pets and they seem to love us. It is certainly less complicated. You can love building bridges with animals, but it they are not the same as those with fellow human beings.

You should make your best effort not to regret things, or not to do things that you may regret. However, the opposite side of guilt is pleasure. One of the things you regret, you may have enjoyed. That is problematical. How you solve that conundrum, I only offer this advice: Life is short so try to have and savor joyful moments. You can regret that you didn't do enough things to regret. There have been many good people who did things that may have been selfish pursuits of personal joy or gratification of some urge. Did that make them bad people? No. It is a dilemma. Sorry, you will have to figure that one out for yourselves.

In the Jewish religion, with the destruction of the second temple by the Romans, the priesthood (Cohen's) went away. Jewish spiritual leaders now have the title Rabbi. It actually means teacher. So these Rabbis offer sage counsel and advice, but it is then up to you to interpret and follow or not follow such advice. You are part of the process on the road of life for the evolution of the planet, in sociological and genetic terms, whether you choose to be or not (uh oh, the big E word again —Existentialism). You add your combined knowledge and influence experiences in the system. The adage that nothing is free is not quite true. What is free is the collective knowledge and the current state of the physical planet that you acquire, once you are born on Earth. You get that system as it is, and then you learn about it and interact with it. Even if you do not write a symphony at seven years old like Mozart, you have an impact on people and things. I greatly suggest that if you are happy, you will impart happiness. Conversely, you can impart great unhappiness. This may ultimately lead to good things, just as other bad things lead to great discoveries. However, why add any more problems; there are enough as it is. There are noble pursuits that I feel I should get around to, like Peace Corp work. There is also a great contribution when you create entertainment in toys, games, movies, jokes, stories, books or other things that make people's lives better, happier, or just cause them to laugh. Sometimes you can make people laugh at horrible things and that has an element of absurdity in it. However, a laugh is a laugh. For those moments, even if you had terminal cancer, you would still be enjoying yourself. Jewish tradition says that all that you do affects future generations. Oye, talk about guilt, eh? It also teaches that you should do things because they are right, not because you fear the wrath of God.

You should try to, and succeed in, enjoying yourself. This does not mean, merely to do things you enjoy, it signifies to figure out how indeed to enjoy—yourself, get it? I am not religious but I have read some books about ancient Jewish philosophy. Let us ignore whether there is God or not for this anecdote. So here goes: Since God made the earth and everything in it, he made many things for his humans to enjoy, like flowers, or grapes, or therefore wine, (perhaps other plants and derivatives, if you want to go that direction) sunny days, snow, mountains, oceans, the ability to be inventive (thinking) to do things like music, learning, medicine, teaching, gardening, sunrise, sunset, fishing, beaches, penguins in Antarctica. He also made men and women so they would not only care for each other and procreate, but that they would enjoy each other. Okay so enjoy each other. You do have to separate use from over indulgence or abuse for all your pursuits. So when you may be standing in judgment by the big guy/girl/person/being, a great sin (if there is sin, if there is God,—E word again), is therefore to not have enjoyed God's works. He gave you these things so how ungrateful (sinful) are you if you do not enjoy them. This is for parable use only. Do not be turned off by my use of this method, please. How interesting, funny, and absurd, that a horrendous sin can in fact be to not do and enjoy some things that other people would consider to be sinful to do and enjoy.

On the subject of happiness, Thomas Jefferson, although enigmatic and contradictory, was a brilliant man. I particularly like the inalienable (great word) right to the pursuit of happiness. Remember, you are not guaranteed happiness, only that you are free to pursue it.

As I get older, I find that because other people have worse than the headache I joked about earlier; helping others is one of the great things to do, even if I don't always practice what I preach.

So what have been my life's experiences and joyful moments that make me credentialed to offer advice? Well, why not?

Life's good experiences:

I have experienced love, and sex (together or separately) and they are both things I heartily recommend. I went to many rock concerts, but also attended some symphony concerts that were great. Music can definitely lift the spirit to soar. It can bring me to laugh, cry, feel great, feel depressed. Music is also something, if you can make it, that comes from somewhere deep in your psyche. Music, it is said, tames the savage beast. Music is a common denominator of all humankind. A guitar teacher told me that everyone has rhythm. The first and primary one is the beating of your heart. Cool guy!

Rock concerts:

Beginning in the 1960's rock concerts started becoming very social events in small venues. You could stand and dance near the stage and see The Doors, Jimi Hendrix, Janis Joplin, Jefferson Airplane, the Grateful Dead, right up close. Certainly, there was the smell of cannabis in the air, but it was not a prerequisite for the experience. The Grateful Dead carried this onward until 1995 when Jerry Garcia died. They always allowed people to record their music free with no lawsuits nor royalty disputes—imagine that! The spirit of this was incredible. People wrote set lists and traded music for decades. If you wanted to spin around, there was a special section for that. Thousands of people dancing in their seats was a spirit and experience that was remarkable. If you want the taste and feel of the 60's musical experience, amazingly, it still exists! Go to see a concert by the Dark Star Orchestra (DSO). They have been touring for years now, doing Grateful Dead concerts in their entirety. At the end of each concert, they announce what venue and year it was. Tickets are twenty some dollars, and they do it in small theatres. They are so accurate that Bob Weir said they are scary. You can stand near the stage, and everyone knows the songs and they dance to them. Most of their audience is too young to have seen the Grateful Dead but they know all the words to all the songs. It is not just a simulation and a tribute band. The spirit, the music, the people are all very accurate and extremely fun even if you do not particularly like that type of music. There are even people selling hand made crafts outside. Check it out. (This is not an infomercial.) This really will give you a clue as to what the 60's spirit was and why it was so appealing.

I did a lot of self-medicating (drug use) in my youth. Since Clinton, Bush, and now Obama, it is okay to admit this. It seemed like it was "cool" at the time (we said "far out" and then "neat" rather than cool.). It did provide euphoria and was helpful for a number of seductions. It initiated camaraderie and I enjoyed myself. With rock concerts, it was also a lot of fun. Unfortunately, ultimately, the pursuit of the highs of the pharmacology, outweighed the good parts with too much use of certain chemicals. This caused me to waste a great deal of precious time that I wish I had back, not to mention large quantities of money; perhaps I should list this in the bad experiences section also. It is interesting to note that Paul McCartney from the Beatles said he does not advocate drug use but he said that the Beatles did some of their best work during their drug use period.

I love dangerous roads for four wheel driving. SCUBA diving is thrilling. Snow skiing downhill through the trees gets my juices going. I cannot recommend enough moments with your children. I have joy when they show unfettered happiness and call me Daddy. Watch a beautiful sunset. Ponder the moon. That one is really good because it gives you a sense of who and where you are. Ranting about cool information I had just learned or accumulated is one of my passions (DUH—hey you are reading this).

I lived outside the USA in mainland China, Colombia, Peru, and Argentina. I definitely recommend living in another country for a while. You get an incredible feeling of accomplishment when you can rely on yourself to function in a different culture, in a different language. Also traveling in general is great. Different parts of the planet are worth seeing. I saw Mt. Everest, Pagan Burma, Tierra Del Fuego, the Great Wall, Mt. McKinley, Chichen Itza, Machu Picchu. In case you have not noticed, I am an endorphin junkie.

Sex:

Ok, what else about sex? If this is truly to be a guide of how to live, I will make a few remarks. Definitely avoid worrying about it while you are doing it. Enjoy yourself, and the other person and try to have your partner do the same. Then there is the Woody Allen joke about doing it with yourself, at least it is with someone you love; well just don't feel bad about it but do get out and do it with someone else once in a while. In the book Shogun by James Calvell, some Japanese Geishas are assigned by the chief of the Japanese clan to "please" the very proper English gentleman sea captain. He declines all of their offers, and they do not understand why the Englishman will not sleep with them. They discuss this and hypothesize about him. They wonder if he may like boys or sheep or geese. On this subject, a lady I met once said, "Whatever blows your skirt up." Consequently, I say, "If you are not hurting someone else, and you are not making yourself feel bad, hey, life is short." Leave me out of this one; I am not making recommendations except to say, "Judge not lest ye be judged".

General enjoyment of things:

Something I learned that exists in much of the rest of the world, that is sorely lacking in America is the simple joy of life. In other countries, people sit in open cafes and drink and eat and talk and watch the world go by. They dance at parties and laugh and sing without worrying about being "nerdy". We have lost that in America. We worry about what people think about us too much. Although I do not advocate cheating on your spouse, I will tell you what a fellow worker said to me when I was working overseas. He told me they were happy to have Americans working for them in Peru. I was proud and smiled and thanked him until he continued. "They spend too much time chasing money and not enough time chasing women." He was quite serious and my smile dropped. So more of my advice is to chase something else besides money.

Lastly, on the subject of sex, I am not ashamed to say that I have been in brothels in Thailand, Indonesia, Colombia, and Peru. It may be sexist for men to indulge themselves that way and it is a sad thing for women to do, but for men it can provide comfort, as Paul Simon said about Seventh Avenue in NYC, or it just can satisfy the libido without a relationship. The two strongest urges to an animal are survival and then mating. So, "Whadaya gonna do, huh?" The oldest profession will probably never go away. I apologize to the women reading this, but it is part of what I know and did and enjoyed. None of you has to agree with my list, I am just indicating my life's experiences and how they seem to have contributed to my thinking. Ladies, in Bangkok, Thailand, you can legally go to the equivalent places for women. So if that blows your skirt up, get an airplane ticket. Of course, you could just go to Las Vegas and let it stay in Vegas. No amount of laws will ever change this. So why bother? Well that is another discussion.

What has this to do with existentialism? That which makes me me or you you, can have meaning and purpose to you, if you interpret them as being significant for you or your family or someone else or the world at large or something else. I am using them as illustrations for your reflection to use to improve your way along the path. What I have done or think may be utterly without purpose in a cosmological context or a sociological context, but still may have purpose in giving me and possibly you, peace of mind. One of my favorite expressions is, "What price, piece of mind". Another expression that everyone uses, which becomes more true with time passing is, "It's only money." Certainly, money is very necessary and its absence or dearth causes unhappiness, but one thing you cannot buy is time. Do things to allow you to feel you took best advantage of your time in life. If it happens, try not to feel guilty for sleeping away a weekend here and there. Remember that you only have a certain number of weekends with your health, walking this planet. Beware! You never know when you will get to know (or not have conscious knowledge) about the great beyond. "The future's uncertain and the end is always near" said Jim Morrison of The Doors.

What you do with your life does not have to have a profound impact on the world to be significant. That you had children means you did something original. Anything that you do day to day may influence any number of other things or people in ways you cannot ever know. This is the "Butterfly Effect."

Life's bad experiences:

Spending a night in jail, although in a weird way it was a good experience. Watching someone you love die is awful in both the original definition of causing you to be full of awe, and the current definition of terrible. Chemistry exams I found simply terrifying. Being sick and in pain is miserable. Staying in a bad relationship too long was a mistake I repeated a few times. One that I believe is very important to avoid is hurting someone physically or emotionally due to carelessness or insensitivity. Disappointing a child makes me feel bad about myself. I wish I were better at forgiving myself. I can walk down the street and slap myself in the forehead with my hand, and berate myself, thinking about something I did or did not do decades earlier.

Regrets:

At Brown, I should have studied harder and my advice is to get an advanced degree. It may be difficult, annoying and seem superfluous, but since you have decided to live in this world (you certainly can depart life at any moment you chose—E word) living by the rules that will pragmatically achieve more degrees of freedom, is a good idea. I regret abandoning learning the piano. A big regret for me is not having played with my children enough, seemingly preferring to worry about work or resolving personal conflicts instead. It sets a bad example for them, and those are priceless precious moments that are lost forever. This is huge. Do not do it!

For me one of the very biggest regrets is disappointing myself when I had an opportunity and I was too timid to act on it. Opportunity knocks unexpectedly. Try not to always make the cautious and safe decision. Once in a while take a chance. Give your self a jolt to your psyche. As metaphors go—steal a kiss; you may get slapped, but then again, you may not. At least you tried. You will never know what a daring move might do for you. I suppose it does not have to be very daring, it may just be uncharacteristic. This change might set you off in an amazing new direction or at least break up a repeating pattern in which you are stuck. Certainly if you never take a chance, nothing will change. Your chance taking does not have to be too outrageous like getting on an airplane to a foreign land, or jumping out of an airplane with a parachute, or yes, literally stealing a kiss. You may love living where you are and have no need or desire to see penguins in Antarctica. For you an uncharacteristic thing could be just to go see something, do something, or read something that you have not tried before. Get up and walk somewhere you have not been. Do not let those weekends go by just "sleeping" Sleeping could be figurative for repeating yourself for decades, and then you wonder where the time went. Then it is too late.

Inter-personal relationships:

The Golden Rule is the best guide. Be compassionate. Say I love you when you should for those relationships. Be kind. Avoid lying. Be evasive if you must, but avoid lying. It makes you feel bad and getting caught makes someone else feel bad and your credibility will be worthless. A problem you will find, if you have not already, is that you are in a position where you do not want to lie, but by telling the truth, you will hurt someone else. Good luck on that one. With children, a lie may not seem like a lie, but it ends up teaching a bad lesson. For example, a child asks you to do something or go somewhere, and you answer, "No we can't. We can go tomorrow". Then when tomorrow comes and you do not go for some reason or another, either the lesson you taught is how to get out of things by saying something that is expedient and may not be true. Is that lying? Sometimes it is. Something else to do is to take a cue from a cat or dog. They like contact with you. You obviously have to be careful with this, but hug your child or spouse or parent, or friend, at least once in a while.

Anger and hostility:

Stand up for yourself. Try however, to be diplomatic. Do not swear at someone in anger. Whatever you are speaking about, and however correct you may be, suddenly all they will hear is F or A, or another one of those words and will assume the posture of righteous indignation. You then will lose. Defeat them with cogent sentences. If you must defend yourself physically, the survival instinct is not one to suppress at that moment. On anger, it is all right to get angry or disappointed. Just try not to dwell on those feelings too long because then they will interfere with other positive things in your life.

Work:

For some lucky people their work is their passion. Keith Richards of the Rolling Stones said he never made a living from anything except his guitar. He also said that your passion is not your passion if you have to force yourself to do it. Some doctors love being doctors. Some businesspersons love the game of sales and marketing, and so forth. In any profession or job, it is very fortunate if you really like it. Okay, then there are many other feelings people have about work. If you find yourself working at a job or for someone you do not care for, or marginally so, I offer this: You may quit and then find yet another job or person you do not like. Do not do this repeatedly as a solution. Look to see if you may be doing the wrong thing. Concerning your fellow workers, be nice to people on the way up, you may meet them on the way down. (My Dad told me that). Do not burn bridges. If you are tempted to quit in anger, or just tell someone off, you may shut the door to a future opportunity. Not doing that allowed me to work overseas after I was laid off during an oil business recession. Lastly, I have found that whatever you do, if you do a good job, even if you do not like what you are doing, you will get raises, praises, promotions, and be left alone. Plan B is not getting those things or worse. That way, if you decide to leave you do it on your terms and leave with a positive feeling and maybe a letter of recommendation. One thing never to do is to tell anyone how much you make. This is pretty hard and fast. All you will get is hurt feelings (theirs or yours) and you could get yourself fired.

Guardianship:

Be a good steward of those things within your control. This includes pets, children, employees, spouses or it could be the environment. Although I am not very philanthropic, I believe giving to the less fortunate is the right thing to do. That makes you and the recipients of your largesse feel better. Actually anything you do that helps someone or something and makes you and he/she/it feel better is a good thing to do. If you want to be existentialist about it, it may not matter, but if it makes you feel good and you impacted the world positively, one of the headaches I referenced earlier, may go away. In other words, you succeeded in accomplishing all of what this book is trying to teach.

Existential dilemma—Right and Wrong:

My definition of good and bad in the things I described above should be self-evident or at least learned from thousands of years of successes, or failures, mistakes and consequences. But people have different opinions especially as befits different cultures and religions. From those differences, in their extreme forms we can end up with all those terrible things that result in degrading the quality of life with pain, suffering and death. Meaningless cosmologically or not, this for me is wrong.

There is also random horror and how to deal with it. Craziness and mass hysteria are horrific. Adolf Hitler, Joseph Stalin, MaoTse Dung, Pol Pot, Papa Doc, Jim Jones, John Wayne Gacey were real people and caused millions and millions of people to die unnecessarily. For the world, did that matter? Ask anyone who remembers it or lost someone or part of themselves, or part of their ability to feel good. Or just ask someone who is aware of it and believes it happened. Then there are natural disasters that kill thousands of people. Why do these things happen? How can we prevent them? Some look to God for answers. That may be comforting, but will not change anything. Pragmatism dictates we must get along somehow using our minds and hearts to solve problems. So praying if you are religious is not the answer, if you are also going to go with the "God helps those who help themselves" notion. I may be part of the answer in helping you to feel better. Religion should be something that comforts you and others. Those that use it as a justification to commit violent acts are misguided. If there is God, I cannot imagine that violence is something he or she wants humans to do against each other.

Conclusions:

Do unto others as you would have them do unto you.

—*Some say God, Some say Moses, others?*

Not making a decision is indeed making a decision.

—*Walter Greenberg*

Life goes on within you and without you

> —*George Harrison, The Beatles*

Until I die this space is occupied.

> —*Ray Davies, The Kinks*

What do you send a sick florist in the hospital?

> —*Soupy Sales*

About Walter Jay Greenberg:

On October 14, 1950, my mother Margery Elizabeth Greenberg (of Dutch descent—Jacobson/Vandenberg) gave birth to me in Pittsburgh Pennsylvania. My father was Herbert Julius Greenberg, of Russian/Ukrainian descent—Ossofyetski, later Greenberg). They met at Brown University where he got a PhD in Applied Mathematics, and she got a Masters degree in English Literature during World War II. (My father's brother Stanley went to Brown as well—and became a screenwriter). My father was mostly a college professor, although he pioneered teaching machines at IBM. My mother became the chairman of a foundation dedicated to issues of abnormal child psychology.

We moved a lot as he got better or different jobs. Dad was a math genius who went to college when he was fourteen years old. Something I think I learned from all this moving around was that if you wait long enough, you could get out of anything. This was comforting and, for some things, helped me and for others, interfered, for example with my assimilation into the fabric of reality. My earliest recollection is of sitting on some stairs in Pittsburgh, feeling alone and sad. Later, after I read Crime and Punishment, I thought of myself as Raskalikoff with the weight of the world on my shoulders—but I could handle it!

When someone says, "Where did you grow up?" I say Denver, Colorado. We moved there in 1965. I still have a few very good friends from there and that seems like home. I did not, at first, live there very long either, inasmuch as I went off to Brown University, between 1968 and 1972. I went to graduate school in geophysics, mineral economics, business, and tried education, but never did get another degree. I went into oil exploration and stuck with that for twenty years, working mostly in the USA, but between1986 and 1991, I went abroad to China, Colombia, Peru, and Argentina. Then I went to work for a family business in Peoria, Illinois where I was the Comptroller and Vice President until the STIHL factory, cancelled our contract in 2008. Now what will I become? Hey, maybe an author.

I have a wife of twenty years, Kathleen Mary, formerly Joynt (Irish/Norwegian). I have a daughter Anna in the terrible teen years, and an eight year old adopted daughter Rosie who is a delight, but hyperactive and quite a bundle. I can and do go on at length. I tend to have to ask people if they want the long or the short version, and I find I need to self modulate as I find myself rambling and digressing. It seems I have ADHD and that is both a curse and a blessing. The curse is my attention has been fractionated throughout my life, and that may be why I did not stick with things academically (that is what my mom says). The blessing is that I am a sponge to information both input and output. I can and do mentally catalogue vast and diverse amounts of information.

Recently I was asked what I thought my greatest accomplishment was—what I was most proud of. This was in an application to be on the TV reality show, "Survivor". I answered, "Imparting information." I impart, therefore I am.

9. Medical Existentialism

by Dr. Laurie Margolies

In preparation for the writing of this chapter, I tried to find a concise definition of existentialism that I could use as the foundation upon which I could focus.

The more I learned about existentialism the more parallels become apparent between existentialism and breast cancer, the disease that I spend my working life detecting and diagnosing. This Chapter discusses an approach to cancer, but nothing in it should be construed as medical advice. Each and every patient is different and unique in her own way.

The existentialist believes that life cannot be fully satisfying and complete because each individual suffers. Every person has a loss and is not perfect; we all lack power over our health and therefore we all lack power over a critical part of our lives. Does this mean our lives are worthless—of course not. Even with the stresses of our suffering, we can feel joy and find meaning in our lives. The existentialist approach to breast cancer can be thought of as the journey to find meaning within the context of cancer's intrusion into our lives. Furthermore, the existentialist might argue that each of us brings a bias and limited objectivity to the diagnosis and treatment of cancer. One might continue the argument to assert that an individual's choices are superior to those of a detached observer. Perhaps, one is never more of an existentialist than when one is fighting for their own health or their very existence.

Although, the anecdotes and examples I will use come largely from my role as a breast imager, you can easily substitute any form of cancer or other serious illness and create similar vignettes.

Screening mammography is a stress that many if not most women over the age of 40 in the United States have experienced once if not multiple times. The stress of the mammogram is not limited to the wait for the procedure and the associated discomfort, but the bane of the worried well is the wait for the answer. Will the mammogram reveal a biological abnormality—or possible abnormality—that will have a significant impact on one's existence, one's freedom and one's life choices?

Consider the case of 40-year-old women who believes herself to be healthy. At the urging of her primary care physician and in keeping with recommending guidelines, she presents to a radiologist's office for a screening mammogram. This happens thousands of times in a day in the United States. The woman is stressed—she has lost control over her life. How long will the mammogram take? How uncomfortable will it be? When will the results be available?

In our hypothetical case (based on real life experiences), the technologist performing the exam notes an abnormality when she is checking the images and brings the exam to the top of the radiologist's queue. He or she talks to the patient, performs some more imaging and ultimately a biopsy. It has now been three hours (or three days) since the time of the screening mammogram appointment; the women has gone from being a healthy woman concerned about her career to a probable cancer patient worried about her survival and the effect of her diagnosis and treatment on her own life as well as on the lives of her children and family.

No one who has not been in that situation can fully comprehend what the individual faces while awaiting the biopsy result. The most important question in many biopsy patients is "Why me?" (Which I assume has led to the Y-Me organization). Existentialists argue that a rational reason is desirable, but often not possible. In the breast cancer scenario, most patients who have this cancer do not have a clear, definable rational cause. Most breast cancer patients do not have a family history of breast cancer. Science has yet to be able to determine why many individuals have breast cancer. Only a relatively small percentage of those with breast cancer are able to say that their cancer is due to a specific DNA mutation. So, the important question of "Why me" is not answerable by science.

The woman who has just received the diagnosis of breast cancer has lost power over part of her life. She now knows that there are cells within her breasts that have broken free of normal control mechanisms and threaten her. Depending upon the pathology, the threat may be due to time—time needed for doctors' appointments and treatment; the threat may also be the continued existence of all or part of one or both breasts or the threat may be to life itself.

The breast cancer diagnosis forces one to make choices. Chemotherapy? What kind? Radiation therapy? What kind? Surgery? What kind? What doctors? Where? When? Existentialism argues that one has the responsibility to make those choices for ourselves. The choices cannot be delegated to another; science is limited and cannot be relied upon to fix everything.

So let us consider the case of the 42 year old professional who has had a biopsy and told that she has a small cancer, but that her family history and biopsy findings put her at risk for more breast cancers. Modern science would say that the risk of this woman having another breast cancer is as close to 100% as anything can be in medicine. What is the existentialist approach? There is no one answer, but I think many existentialists would argue that a woman is never better than when she is fighting against their body and fighting for her life.

The breast cancer patient faces many choices. One choice is whom to tell about the diagnosis. Some women let as many people as possible know about their diagnosis and call on friends and family for help getting to appointments and keeping up with "normal" daily activities. Many women work a full schedule while getting breast cancer treatment. Others, not all, continue on as if almost nothing has changed, but join Breast Cancer support groups and help others through the process. Others engage in fund raising for breast cancer research. And yet others, tell almost nobody—not even their sisters or mothers. They suffer in relative silence asking for help from no one. Free will allows a woman to choose any option and to change options along the way. The choices one makes are stressful and have consequences for the woman and her family. But, there is no right or wrong choice when there is no true rational reason for making a certain decision. The rules are arbitrary and changing. Medical science is changing. Social science is changing. Life itself is changing. Existential philosophy recognizes all of the foregoing affirmations.

As a young doctor in training, I had the privilege of meeting a physician who told me her own story. She was a surgeon who had a strong family history of breast cancer. She did her own research and her own soul searching and determined that the only way she could attempt to beat the odds was to have a prophylactic bilateral mastectomy, i.e. have both of her breasts removed. It made sense to her, but not to the many physicians she consulted about having this done. No one would perform the surgery. When I met her she had breast cancer that had metastasized to her bones and she died of breast cancer. Times have changed and prophylactic mastectomies are now considered a reasonable procedure by many and are offered to a select group of patients.

Existentialism objects to the imposition of beliefs or values on the individual in situations similar to the above example. I believe the existentialist would have argued that the woman's free will and choices should have been supported. It was, the existentialist would argue, society's value system that placed keeping a woman intact above her health. The refusal to accede to her request destroyed her health, was in and of its self dehumanizing and robbed her of free will and eventually her life.

How often to have screening mammograms, whether or not to have screening breast ultrasounds or screening breast MRI studies, whether to have a lumpectomy or mastectomy, whether to have partial or full breast irradiation and when and what kind of chemotherapy to have are all questions that face women every day. Existentialism argues that making these stressful decisions is an important part of life's journey. It is not what an individual chooses so much as how they go about the choice that defines the person's nature. The stresses on an individual as well as her own circumstances, affect her ability to make rational choices and consequently affects the choices themselves. What is the cost? Cost in dollars? In time? In side effects? How will others react to the choice? Is there an objective best choice? Ultimately, each person is responsible for making those choices that best suit him or her.

Laurie Margolies, M.D., first studied existentialism as a bio-medical ethics concentrator at Brown University. She then went on to study medicine at Yale University and trained in radiology at Columbia and Yale. After many years in the private practice of radiology she is now fulfilling her dream of practicing academic breast imaging at the Mount Sinai School of Medicine where she is involved in directing patient care, teaching and breast imaging research. Dr. Margolies has been active in the New Haven County Medical Association, the American College of Radiology and The Brown University Schools Program.

10. Simply and Profoundly Christy

by Christy Ann Welty

> Believe nothing,
> No matter where you read it, or who said it,
> No matter if I have said it,
> Unless it agrees with your own reason and your
> own common sense.[1]

[1] My favorite quote is attributed to Buddha (Hindu Prince Siddhartha, or Gautama Buddha, the founder of Buddhism, circa 563-483 B.C.). Coming down through many generations and languages of oral tradition (from Sanskrit to many local languages and dialects) and then through written translations from Karosthi through several languages and finally to English, how accurately could this quote actually capture what Buddha said? No problem. The message itself sets the exercise of quoting on its head if one is quoting to inform or persuade (unless one is debating the very nature of the person being quoted). In my opinion, quotes are useful for entertaining or embellishing, for flavoring or condensing, but they're not useful as a substitute for "your own reason and your own common sense." So my favorite quote renders quotes irrelevant except as ornamentation, which, far from being irrelevant, is quite an important activity for any artist. "...[B]eauty is its own excuse for being." (Ralph Waldo Emerson) or, "Delight is a good excuse for decorating with bright, shiny objects." (Christy Ann Welty) "Or cute, little wingdings." (Ibid.)

That being said, I will proceed to present my conclusions without strict attention to proof, because the proofs you need will necessarily come from *your* experience, not mine or someone else's. Either you will have an experience or revelation that supports my offering and then we'll agree, or you won't have and we'll not. So it goes.

Human nature is robust. We humans have been behaving with the same basic make-up for millennia, so I have nothing new to say about psychology that hasn't already been said by thousands of sages throughout the ages, and dozens of well-known, well-respected wise ones of our modern times, plus umpteen billions of mothers and fathers. But I'll say them anyway, because I remember reading and hearing these ideas dozens of times, maybe hundreds of times, yet for each message there was a singular point of time when it clicked. That point was the nexus—the time when I was ready for the message and the message was ready for me.

> Printed on paper from writer to reader,
> Pendant in ether tween giver, receiver,
> Here now we be, with messages three,
> Nexus alleged awaits our decree.

These headlines (or bumper stickers) capture the top three lessons of my life in ten words:

Gratitude Defeats Depression
Reality Beats Suffering
Happiness Hot in Trials

That's the chapter outline—those three points. A champion of legends, "Reality Beats Suffering" captures the whole of existential psychology. It is broad enough to apply to everyone at all times in all places. The other points highlight two important personal revelations for me, and of course, in my opinion,

everyone would benefit from digesting these nuggets (or chest-
nuts, as the case may be)—that's why I picked 'em!

Gratitude Defeats Depression

> You can't be depressed and grateful at the same time.[2]

"Count your blessings." "Show some gratitude." "Thank God!"
These reminders to be grateful are not enough to counteract
sadness, grief, or periods of mourning. However, the deeper one
penetrates each side, the down side and the thankful side, the
further these feelings diverge. At some point, deep-seated
depression is overcome and healed by an ongoing growth of
gratitude.

I remember several years ago knowing gratitude only as an
intellectual concept —an insipid, hackneyed bromide. Of
course I could count my blessings—one, two, three, and hundreds more—who couldn't do that? Gratitude as an intellectual
exercise, as a calculation of credits, does yield some benefit, but
not the magical kind that suffuses your being with serenity.
That kind of serenity defeats not only depression, but most of
the ills of humanity. Worry, spite, bitterness, conceit, and fear
vanish like mist when simple, humble gratitude glows in your
soul.

This may be explained by brain studies done by scientists
who say they have found that genuine feelings of gratitude and
appreciation release oxytocin and serotonin, two hormones

[2] In his book, *How to Heal Depression*, Peter McWilliams attributes this
quote to Randall Miller. I know nothing of Randall Miller except for this
quote, but having seen it attributed, I'll continue the credit. I have said the
same thing myself many times, as have others, I'm sure.

which act as natural anti-depressants in your body and brain. That's where some of the feeling of suffusion of serenity comes from. But don't try to fake it. According to brain scientists, faking appreciation is stressful and raises levels of cortisol, a stress hormone which causes the opposite effect. (The next section of this chapter shows that fakery causes suffering.)

Developing your sense of gratitude is probably the single most effective approach to improving your mental and physical health, spirituality, and overall happiness. That's quite a mouthful, because it puts the influence of gratitude ahead of the highly acclaimed trio of exercise, diet, and sleep. I contend that gratitude is the foundation which makes it easier for you to support the elements of that trio plus other life-enhancing practices, too.

For all its importance as a linchpin of better living, gratitude is amazingly accessible. For beginners, it can be practiced as a skill, like physical training. As one gains experience, the exercises become more subtle and the effects more sublime. Once started in the conscientious practice of gratitude, steps toward further evolution present themselves without much trouble. Maybe you are already a long way down that path. If so, congratulations and good for you! But there are beginners who need to get started. This section is for them.

Personal story about three fundamentals: please, thanks, sorry

I grew up in a household where please, thank you, and sorry were almost never used among family members. It wasn't because we disliked each other or were unaware of those social graces. We used those words with outsiders, not the people we spent most of our time with. My father considered such phrases to be anachronistic, excessive, and obsequious—in a word—silly. He argued that mannerly phrases were anachronistic because we were supposed to be modern and iconoclastic and not in thrall to tradition for its own sake. They were excessive because they served no basic utility. The model of efficient communication was a computer network, which doesn't use superfluous language in its communications between nodes. Obsequious behavior was overtly reviled, and considered not just silly but dangerous. We were raised to be individuals of pride, honor, and self-sufficiency, not bowing nor scraping to any authority but the family leader. Using words like please, thank you, and sorry was too deferential in his opinion—they sullied the lofty idealism of self-reliance and independence.[3] At the time I thought this approach to personal communication might be kind of quirky, but not really detrimental.

I moved on and married, but kept that old ungrateful habit of speech. Then I discovered the value of gratitude, and decided to conscientiously culture the habit[4] of using please, thank you, and sorry at home with my husband. It was awkward at first, but soon it became easy and fun and it *felt good*. Some guardedness thawed (I hadn't even known it was there!) and it became easy to smile during exchanges of those silly little words.

Now here's the kicker. My mother and father had since divorced but each had carried along the habit of not saying the "silly" words. When I visited either of them, I found that my new habit, now so easy in my own home, stalled. The words literally stuck in my throat—with lips ready and sounds cued up …nothing came out. It was the weirdest feeling, as if the atmospheric pressure of the house conspired to push against the surge of grateful speech. And when the words stuck, the flow stopped, and something went rigid, like a hard steel rod between my tongue and diaphragm. Disturbed and uncomfortable, I realized that excising "silly" words was not just quirky; it was indeed

[3] To be "obsequious" is to act with servile deference, and "deference" can indicate submission, but "deferential" can also be synonymous with "respectful." "Obsequious" is not the same as "respectful," and I would propose that while obsequiousness endeavors to give the appearance of respect, it also signals latent hostility on some level.

[4] This is the first exercise for enhancing one's sense of gratitude.

detrimental to the emotional health of family members. It seems to me that when the flow of gratitude between human beings is impeded, loneliness and misery set anchor in the darkness of unexamined thoughts and emotions.

The flow of gratitude between people is important, yes, but the more important flow can be harder to notice because it flows within oneself. Its channel is between the two organs of the mind: the heart and brain. I think this is why I felt the steel rod between my diaphragm and tongue—between heart and brain.

Point of practice for good mental hygiene: using the magic words

Children are often trained to use the words, "Please," "Thank you," and "I'm sorry," rather mechanically. After a child's request for a cookie, for example, an adult might hold it just out of reach of a child's hand, saying, "What's the magic word?" as if "please" is a token dropped into the ear-slot to turn the brain-cog so the prize drops down on the arm-lever. Perhaps the adult thinks, yes, that is exactly how "please" works!

In other situations, you've probably seen a child receive something and heard from an accompanying adult, "Now what do you say?" as if "thank you" is an audible token that rolls down the tongue-chute at the end of an exchange—ka-ching!

It might be lucky that apology is the rarest of the three situations, because training a child to apologize is tough. "Say you're sorry," says an adult, who may end the training session as soon as the child's mouth emits the expected syllables with a sufficient decibel level, even if the emission carries hostility or fails to carry regret, remorse, or sympathy.

It's hard to say which is worse—growing up with an injunction against using these words or being trained to use them mechanically. In either case, your goal now is to invoke their utmost value, to let them infuse your daily interactions with the goodness of their real magic.

I devote some detail to "please" here as an example of these words. "Thank you" and "sorry" have their own flavors but follow the same general formula as "please": expressing respect for the other and for oneself; practicing humility and detachment; empowering both other and self; and increasing intimacy between the two. These four features benefit the individual psychology of both self and other at any level of sincere conversation. They grace our brief exchanges with good cheer, and they can be developed to levels of unutterable profundity between close friends.

Before you say anything

Any word or phrase can be altered by your tone of voice and other innuendos to send a hundred different meanings. To choose the right shade for your situation, the first point is to be honest with yourself about your motives. The second point is to be sincere with your listener about your intentions. These two qualifications are deceptively easy—who isn't honest and sincere? The fact is soul-searching is an endless and challenging journey, so we do our best as we go along. After you are clear with your purpose, it's time to convey it with words, some of which might be "magic."

Magic words are special because they belong only in certain kinds of messages: those which are honest and sincere PLUS kind and respectful. Coming round full circle in a bizarre inversion of the theme, sometimes honest, sincere messages are conveyed with such utter kindness and respect that magic words become redundant and superfluous. Sometimes words themselves are redundant and superfluous and actually bog down the tenderness and subtlety being expressed.

"Please"

The word "please" signals respect for power. The comparable phrase in French is, "s'il vous plait," which literally translates to "if it pleases you," which is a clear reminder that you are asking your listener to grant you a wish—you're not cranking the gears on a machine. Lay your desires at your listener's feet, where she will contemplate them while hearing your plea. You have calculated the risk that, being so close to her feet, your desires could possibly get kicked or crushed. In fact, just before you lay them down, it's a good idea to detach from your desires, to tell them goodbye, to take a moment to mourn their impending extinction, because you are hoping for fulfillment, not forcing fulfillment, and you are aware that you do not control your listener's decision. You have only the power to make your petition pleasing, so you present it with respect for your listener's power to grant your wish or not, and with confidence in your ability to live without its fulfillment.

This approach empowers both of you equally. Sometimes in the heat of desire, you forget that you can live without its fulfillment—you forget you are creative enough to work around a refusal. Detaching from your desire at the moment you voice it reminds you of your inherent power.

In an ironic twist, your detachment actually adds appeal to your presentation at a subtle level. The charming combination of humility and confidence persuades the other soul that you have come in peace, with no intention of attacking, so defensiveness suddenly seems cumbersome and irrelevant. Bare of armor, bereft of their weapons, two souls naked get ready to reckon as fate awaits them with perfect discretion.

What a seductive sound a "please" can be!

"Please" for children

A human starts life as an infantile being who is extremely self-centered and advances from there to discover more and more beings who matter to it. These beings aid a child's development by providing encounters with reality—by expecting the child endure the consequences of its behavior. As a child's trainer, you are its translator of reality. Your explanations and translations give a child some structure to start with, something to modify while going about the job of learning.

Along with explanations describing how and when "please" fits into a social exchange, a child needs object lessons to demonstrate how exchanges actually work beneath the surface (or fail, as the case may be). Here's an example.

"Get me some water, Mother."

"No, thanks."

Pause to digest. "No, Mother, I said, 'Get me some water.'"

"Yes, I heard you, and in response I declined your suggestion. I might add that I declined more politely than you suggested."

The child looks stunned and clueless, especially if this is the first exchange like this.

"But I can't reach the faucet!"

Mother looks at child with appreciation for the unfortunate predicament, and says, "How unfortunate, darling. It would be so much easier for you if somebody found happiness in getting water for you, wouldn't it?"

Child looks crestfallen. "Don't you like to get me water?"

"I feel good about doing things that make us both happy. But when you treat me like your puppet, as if my feelings don't matter to you, then I feel like you should be talking to your puppet, not to me."

Child may feel lost at this point. ["But my puppet can't get me water—you can." "I can if I want to, but you haven't given me much reason to."] If this exchange has happened before, the child may remember to use "please" with the request. If "please" doesn't come to mind, some prompting is needed.

"How do you think you might make your suggestion more attractive to me? Even if you make your suggestion **very** attractive, I still might not want to get you water. In either case, how would you show me that my feelings matter to you?"

In my experience, at this point, the child finally hears something he knows about. Mother may get a big, heartfelt hug and hear, "Your feelings matter to me, Mama."

"Yes, I know, sweetheart," with a big hug in return. Kneeling to get to his level is helpful while you both savor this emotional breakthrough. "Another way to show that my feelings matter to you is to use the word 'please' and then let me have the choice of doing it or not."

Child smiles with relief at the simplicity of the solution.

With a new attitude of contrition and connection, the child asks sweetly, "Would you please get me some water, Mother?" as he smiles with confidence that you certainly could not resist such a charming request. One more thought occurs to him, "And then I'll share it with you!"

Segue: Gratitude + Reality = Optimistic Existentialism

> Let us rise up and be thankful, for if we didn't learn a lot today, at least we learned a little, and if we didn't learn a little, at least we didn't get sick, and if we got sick, at least we didn't die; so, let us all be thankful.[5]

[5]] This quote is also attributed to Buddha—same guy, same caveats.

I used to loath housework. It seemed so pointless, tedious, and dysfunctionally repetitive. It felt like a conspiracy against genius. (Uh, yes, genius. Loathing is a hobby of arrogance.)

Well, I don't do any more housework now than I did then —I do less—but I don't loath it these days. I rather enjoy it, and there are two main reasons for that reversal: first, feeling gratitude, and much later, embracing reality.

Point of practice for stretching the range of emotion: counting blessings

One of the things I hated about housework was that it was a lonely task. Just me and the vacuum cleaner, or me and the dustrag. And the everlasting dust, of course. I indulged in self-pity because it was an easy accompaniment to monotonous tasks. The turnaround happened when the idea clicked that I wasn't alone, far from it. Instead, I discovered a great team working with me.

The vacuum cleaner, for example, was no longer just an awkward, clunky anchor to drag around behind me. Not at all. Instead it became a fine, humming machine, happy to follow along and help with my work by whisking up dust and storing it for me until I was good and ready to change the bag. Somebody, another teammate, had invented that machine long ago, and other unknown teammates had improved the original design. It was ever so handy that I did not have to use my genius to invent that machine. Having it complete and all ready to go was such a blessing. Plus there were all the people at the factory who assembled it, and all the people in the chain of distribution who transported it until it found me. And the parts suppliers, and their distributors. It was mind-boggling to think of the size of the team that had contributed to us working together, that vacuum cleaner and me.

In true team spirit, I started feeling friendly toward the

little tool. Of all things, we were becoming pals. What with the contributions from all those people, plus the willingness and reliability of the little machine to roar to life any time I pushed its button, I actually felt honored to be the point person for the team—the player scoring the goal.

The earthly physical aspect of the team is relatively easy to grasp and practice with. A bit more challenging is the ethereal aspect of teamwork, yet that's where some great rewards lie.

First let me explain that in this chapter I have focused mainly on primary propositions for improving psychological well-being based directly on my experience of bootstrapping out of (non-existential) mud onto an (existential) path. When one has known only the ruts of non-existential mud, the concept of a path is completely intellectual. For all practical purposes, one's mind/body has become unaware of anything but mud. The brain's circuitry, the body's biochemistry, and the mind's experience all are keyed to the mudbath, and it takes the renowned leap of faith to make the passage. In my opinion, the toughest transition is from mud to path. That's why I have put so much emphasis on it—these were major turning points for me which made all the difference.

Once established on the path, it tends to unfold itself before you as long as you keep walking onward one step at a time. A significant part of the path is spiritual—it is indeed your spiritual path. Poised here, then, is the other part of the team, the ethereal spiritual side—slipperier to grasp at first and more elusive to practice with, but gratifying nevertheless, and arrayed with an infinite upside potential.

Though I blessed my earthly team immediately and enthusiastically, my appreciation for the ethereal aspect of the team has taken its time to grow gradually over the years. The aspects that are easiest to identify and define are those which are connected to some earthly manifestation, such as a physical object or a physical action. Some of these, for example, are the intentions of the human team members along with the types of energy they brought to their tasks; the kinetic and potential energies contained among the atoms of the materials of the physical objects; Mother Earth herself, and her climate and weather at the time the vacuum cleaner and I are working together; the sun and its rays of energy streaming through the picture window highlighting airborne motes; the vibrations of the electromagnetic spectrum including the light spectrum we see plus all the hidden spectrums we can't see. There are more forces and more flows, plus there is the ultimate force and the ultimate flow of our universe.

These are my ethereal teammates, and I feel blessed beyond words to be working with them as we chase dustbunnies down the halls.

Point of practice for flexing mental muscle: embrace reality

The reality of housework is that my mother's standards were very different than my own. I suffered, as will be explained in the next section, due to my erroneous assumption that I was failing to meet some preset standard of housework—my mother's, my boyfriend's, my neighbor's—there were so many standards, all much more stringent than were compatible with me.

One day I decided to clean the bathroom fixtures. My motive was to please someone else, to meet my friend's idea of what would be good for me. After scrubbing the tub a few minutes, wracking sobs and streams of tears started wrenching themselves out of me. I figured it was insane to continue cleaning when my body was fighting such a battle against it. So I quit. I decided I had to stop adopting other people's standards and find some of my own. Only then I found peace. (And spiders found a haven keeping insects in check.)

Reality Beats Suffering

Suffering is resistance to what is.

That is the take-away, the six-word summary of how humans handle life on this planet. Most of them suffer. That's why you hear them say, "Life is suffering."[6] Yes, people suffer until they stop resisting the way things are. Then suffering goes away. For a few more words on this subject, here's a quote to chew on.

> Do you want a sign that you're asleep? Here it is: you're suffering. Suffering is a sign that you're out of touch with the truth. Suffering is given to you that you might open your eyes to the truth, that you might understand that there's falsehood somewhere, just as physical pain is given to you so you will understand that there is disease or illness somewhere. Suffering occurs when you clash with reality. When your illusions clash with reality, when your falsehoods clash with truth, then you have suffering. Otherwise there is no suffering.[7]

This philosophy is an excellent guide to better living and a robust early warning system for trouble. It gets me through very bad times, and brings great satisfaction to very good times. I could probably fill a book with personal stories and points of practice related to this theme, but lots of other people have already done that.

[6] Attributed to the caveatted Buddha as a distillation of the first of his "Four Noble Truths."

[7] Anthony de Mello (1931–1987), a Jesuit priest and psychotherapist, also believed that "the greatest human gift is to be aware, to be in touch with oneself, one's body, mind, feelings, thoughts, sensations."

Personal story about aligning with reality

The reality is that my deadline is now, this hour, and this is the end of my third extension. Richard wants this electronic document within minutes but I had had more writing planned for it. So I reduced my plan for the Gratitude section, and wrote only about "please" instead of rambling on for two more sections very similar to the first. We all probably benefited from that edit. And I have to severely reduce my original plan for the second and third sections, Reality and Happiness, and hope that a few nuggets still come through. But then I remember that two quotes inspired me during my roughest emotional challenge—just four sentences. I could cut to the marrow of one quote per each of the last two sections, and my job would be done. Not as fun, perhaps, but it would be perfectly aligned with the essence of the chapter title: it would be simple.

So I'm not going to pull my hair nor gnash my teeth. I'm going to edit.

Happiness Hot in Trials

This headline is a bit cryptic. It refers to the following quote, which I discovered while reeling from a severe emotional blow. It inspired a flicker of hope during a grueling trial, so I copied it onto a slip of paper and carried it around in my wallet so I could take it out and look at it several times a day as my mind was in such a fog I kept forgetting what it said.

> Thousands of candles can be lighted from a single candle, and the life of the candle will not be shortened. Happiness never decreases by being shared.[8]

This little charm saved me from wallowing in an abyss of guilt and shame. It's a formula for deciding how long to beat yourself up over doing something really stupid. How long do you show your friends how bad you feel about your mistake? How long do you display your shame about your faulty judgment? These are not idle questions at any time, and they loom especially large when your life is in shambles and you haven't developed any plans for rebuilding because you're so rattled you don't have enough attention to retain the meaning of two sentences for as long as two minutes. (Or one sentence if it's *that* long.)

The core issue here is that while grief and mourning are natural and healthy, wallowing in an excessive display of despair is definitely unhealthy. So when your natural grieving is done, don't tote around a sad face as if you're groveling and doing penance for bad judgment that has already been tried, sentenced, and settled. You drain your friends when you do that. Dig up a happy thought and put forth a smile—your candle— even when it feels like it might be a lot of hard work to do so. Do the work. Your candle won't feel lessened by sharing its flame with your friends. And the flames of your friends won't feel lessened when you partake of their joys with them. Everyone will feel uplifted, and you'll all deserve it. Really. No matter how stupid you feel inside.

Caveat: There might be some people who expect you to grovel and do excessive penance. Avoid these people. Their behavior is not friendly.

[8] Buddha again, the guy with all the caveats. He may have more than his fair share of quotes when there are so many other people who would have much better documentation available. The author might be revealing bias, or a narrow knowledge base, or a suboptimal search engine, or a lazy streak, or a freak-out due to an editorial deadline. I reckon lots of people, including most spiritual leaders, have said many of the same things Buddha is credited with saying. And Buddha probably said them, too.

Well, folks, that's it. Out of time. Chapter's end. Fare thee well.

As you grow forth, I do hope you find your favorite flower to play with along your path.

Christy Ann Welty is a woman who has given a great many things to a great many people and she has a great deal more that she wishes to accomplish. She has been a highly successful Libertarian political figure and vote getter in Iowa and has been a lifetime proponent of existentialism and libertarian values. A former City Councilwoman, she holds a BSCE in Mathematics and an MS in Mechanical Engineering and is a writer of prose, poetry and political theory. Christy has traveled many paths with some of the other contributors to this work and has brought to all she meets along the way, much happiness and food for thought.

Christy is the mother of two. She currently lives in Fairfield, Iowa.

11. The Endless Road—
Existentialism & Political Freedom

by Ed Noyes, Esq.

I found myself once again with Richard (aka "Butch") on the long road to a distant state to meet others whom, we hoped, would resonate with our "vision". There's something freeing about knowing that there's 1,500 miles plus between you and your destination. Not much to do but to relax, talk and maybe listen to some music. (Lots of time to tell stories, to reveal intimacies about some juicy past, or to contemplate what some paid stooge said on Fox News).

I find that it's very enjoyable, and sometimes enlightening, to just let my mind go. To let it reach out to whatever distance it can and to let it find its own road, and destination. To have the freedom to do this with another like-minded individual is truly a blessing, and, can often lead to some surprising realizations.

Butch and I met as a result of many intersecting paths, most of which we never knew we were on together.

In the fabled Nebraska education system, where I was among the elite in my 37 member class, I was able to easily "skate through" my classes without hardly any effort at all. Believe me when I say that "no child left behind" was alive and well in the early 70's within the American educational system. It's a simple enough concept that places the emphasis on "results" (translated as making sure that everyone passes and resulting in no one (almost ever) truly excelling). The real question was: "who's grading the system and for what purpose"?

I was among that group that had no vision delivered to us, no emphasis on individuality, and no time to foster that unique spark in each student. It was pretty damn easy and exceedingly boring.

Among my favorite classes was English, as I enjoyed new ideas from other kindred souls that had taken the time to attempt communication with someone like me. Even though I loved to read I don't believe I finished more than two or three books during my entire high school career. (I finally figured out years later that I could choose to educate myself, because I WANTED to, instead of education being something that was forced upon me).

The first book I remember that grabbed my attention was "1984" by George Orwell. Because I was always interested in history and public events, what Orwell presented as a possible future for my world shook me to the core. I grew up loving my family, my Nebraska Cornhuskers, and my country as one big red, white and blue vision of superiority and deserved patriotism. Orwell said it could become a nightmare! I remember, at one singular moment, making the first commitment I ever made in my life. I vowed that "if I ever see any of this happening, I would dedicate myself to stopping it!". Little did I know where this vow would lead.

At one point I realized that "If I was ever going to make a difference in the world, I would have to understand how the world actually works". This led me inevitably to attend law school. I was the first in my family's known history to become a lawyer (it's not like anyone directed me to go). It was all part of the "plan" that some cosmic computer figured out (after I made that crazy vow).

Strange books would appear for me to read on laundry mat side tables, such as "None Dare Call It Conspiracy". This book literally blew my mind as it revealed the inner workings of history, the shaping of various educational paradigms, and the mechanics of how history (and the future) can be determined by those who define history itself.

I became a veritable lunatic, intent on discovering "the truth" so that I could make a difference. I uncovered different layers of reality, delving into not only history and politics, but also spiritual dimensions, including meditation practices, natural lifestyles and alternative health.

I'll never forget my friend "Wesley". You don't meet a guy like Wesley everyday. After suffering 3 different serious head injuries as a child Wesley's doctors said he should have half of his brain removed, which apparently was necessary. As a result of having nearly the entire left side of his brain removed, Wesley grew to have unique abilities. Through the over developed right side of his brain, Wesley could (among other abilities) "cognize" the workings of atoms sufficient to ace advanced organic chemistry final exams, without ever going to class! Wesley became my personal advisor on the "inner workings" of the world, which he could "see". Strange stuff, indeed.

I have learned that Nature, or life, has a way of giving you what you seek. "Ask and Ye shall receive," the great master once said. I believe that we all have a "destiny", but that destiny is chosen by each of us on some level. Courage may be the key, as we can all ask for any number of experiences or destinations.

As I write these words I am reminded of a statement my young legal assistant has in all of his emails: Concerning all acts of initiative and creation there is one truth, the ignorance of which kills countless ideas and splendid plans: that the moment one definitely commits oneself, the Providence moves too.

It is obvious to me that "Providence" or whatever you call it "listens" and reacts to support our individual or collective desires. Too many strange coincidences have occurred in my life for me to believe otherwise.

Butch was one of those "blessings" along my path or journey. Prior to meeting Richard (his secret code name deriving from an ironic name an old high school buddy of his had bestowed upon Richard) I felt compelled to offer myself as a "candidate" for public office. This "pre-destined commitment" came after a few years of intently studying the history behind the formation of America with a group of fellow "madmen." We had discovered the original vision of America as a guiding light for the entire world, based on peaceful coexistence, individual liberty and responsibility, and emphasizing the highest virtues of humanity. We felt the passion of Patrick Henry, Thomas Jefferson and James Madison (amongst others) and instinctively wanted to fulfill our roles, as well.

One of my study partners, Clyde Cleveland, felt the same passion I felt that week of August, 2002 (only I was riding a motorcycle in the Black Hills of South Dakota). Clyde concluded that he should run for Governor of Iowa and asked if I would run for Attorney General. Only a lack of courage could have kept me from that choice. Fortunately, I was not alone. (Was it coincidence that on the evening of September 10, 2001 I prayed to God for a "sign" that we were doing the right thing, as we were scheduled to "go public" with a meeting the next evening to announce our candidacies). When I awoke the next morning I was informed that the World Trade Centers had been hit by "terrorists". (We delayed our announcement by one week for things to cool down).

Richard was one of many in the library the night we made our public announcement in Iowa City. We explained our "libertarian" vision and our passion to "restore" America. We spoke from the heart and hoped that someone would listen. The next day we received a call from Richard as he too was interested in pursuing his passion for an outlet of expression. Richard's offer to run as Lieutenant Governor was more than warmly received.

Some would have said that the conclusion of that "run" would have signaled the end of the road for those "wannabees". (At least the Dems and Repubs would like to keep it that way). Others would say that it was only the beginning, or perhaps the beginning of the end.

Passion and commitment have their own out-workings, however. When Butch called me a couple of years later with his "hair-brained" idea to run for Vice President of the United States, I was more than excited. I knew I was still alive, with new challenges, and new opportunities for courage.

I sat comfortably in the rental car next to Richard, zooming to Florida, singing together one of Richard's all time favorite songs: "The Weight" by The Band. One of the stanzas goes like this:

Catch a Cannonball, now, t'take me down the line
My bag is sinkin' low and I do believe it's time.
To get back to Miss Annie, you know she's the only one.
Who sent me here with her regards for everyone.

Take a load off Fannie, take a load for free;
Take a load off Fannie, And (and) (and) you put the load right on me.

We asked ourselves many times what the heck these lyrics meant. We both loved the song. Richard said the lines about "putting the load on me" represented his willingness to "carry the weight" of the Libertarian Party, to carry their mantle, as it were.

It's a beautiful thing when nature rewards you with "signs" of success. As fate would have it, Richard was chosen as the Vice

President candidate for the Libertarian party, pursuant to their elaborate process for picking not only Presidential candidates but the VP candidates as well. He appeared throughout America on the ballot of virtually every state and The District of Columbia, being one of only a handful of Americans to ever accomplish that feat.

As I read the lines now I "see" the following: The words" Catch a cannonball now to take me down the line" represents one's (my) willingness to follow the path of my vision as it is shot out by nature as if a "cannon ball". Catching it "now" represents the present moment (and not just some idea of possible future actions. Following my vision with present moment faith and actions will "take me down the line" towards fulfilling that vision.

"My bag is sinking low and I do believe it's time" symbolizes the unmet needs of the world that "it's time" to address.

"To get back to Miss Annie, you know she's the only one" to me represents my (and others') quest to return American back to Lady Liberty, as she's the only one (liberty) that can save America once again.

"Who sent me here with her regards for everyone" represents the voices from the past, symbolized by Lady Liberty, who still sends us their regards, and well wishes and still show us "the way" to return to our freedom.

I believe Lady Liberty was pointing to a spiritual truth available to all, that some call freedom and others might call existential optimism.

The magnificence of embracing an "existential" reality is that one embraces one's freedom to choose one's own interpretation of reality, personal, political and otherwise. From that choice, one can "choose" to do anything. If that "anything" is inspiring to you, then how much more magnificent is that choice? If that "choice" is supported by "Nature" then the power of the heavens is behind you. One's own quest then becomes part of a cosmic quest. Finally, if one can enjoy the company of other like-minded questers, who can laugh and sing songs together, and dream together, and thereafter work together with joy in their hearts, as we travel down the road together, then truly, we have found our way back home.

Ed Noyes is a talented and passionate attorney and author, specializing in commercial and bankruptcy law. He currently practices in Fairfield, Iowa although he is a born and bred Cornhusker, hailing from a small farm community outside of Lincoln, Nebraska. Ed indefatigably strives to understand the world about him, from every imaginable perspective- personal, philosophical, political and pedagogical. He is the perfect contributor to this book and I am grateful that he took time from his busy law practice to write this chapter on existentialism, politics and the law. He ran for Attorney General of the State of Iowa in 2002 and served as Richard Campagna's campaign manager in 2004, guiding the candidate towards obtaining the Libertarian Party's contested nomination for Vice President of the United States...He continued to advise Campagna throughout the entire arduous general Presidential election of '04.

12. Dos And Don'ts
50 Dos And Don'ts of Existential Reality

according to Richard Campagna

In addition to capturing, digesting, assimilating and effectuating your own personal modifications to the philosophical approach depicted herein, below please find fifty (50) things to do and not to do, which will certainly serve you well in this optimistic, existential world in which we all live. There is no order nor rhyme nor reason to the list, and it is a bit irreverent at times, but implementation of the following list during the course of my own life-span, has worked out quite well for me heretofore. Here we go:

1) Make $1.00 contributions to as many worthy causes as contact you and that you can prudently afford.

2) Play hard to get, even if you must walk away from a few good opportunities from time to time. In the long run, the great opportunities for which you are a wonderful "fit" will chase you down more often than not.

3) To the extent possible, don't defecate in other people's houses. In my youth, two or three of my supposed "idols" did so in

my parents' home and when the toilet got stuck and overflowed, my image of them was "shot." My wife urged me not to include this somewhat "gross" tip in the book but the recollections of the people who didn't follow this guideline still remain so ingrained in my memory that I feel compelled to do so.

4) Don't take yourself too seriously—ever.

5) Whether you need to or not, for minor lending needs, always try family and friends before contacting commercial lending institutions.

6) Develop a great memory, especially for seemingly trivial details regarding the lives of others.

7) Humility must be practical. Don't give in to the temptation of braggartry about your own accomplishments or those of your family members, no matter how appealing its fleeting promise may seem.

8) Say "I love you" as many times to as many people as feels right for you…even when such is difficult.

9) Don't over meddle in the lives of your adult children. Life is changing so fast that even when you think you understand things better than they do, even if you think you're doing the right thing, you probably don't and aren't.

10) Don't be embarrassed to believe in God. There is a God. Of course there is a God!

11) Consider going to law school if you can afford it, even if you never intend to practice. As life gets tougher, a law degree will be a useful tool in defending and protecting your individual and family rights. Alternatively, if financial concerns exist, do not go to law school unless there are other compelling reasons for doing so.

12) If you are a baby boomer like I am and were lucky enough to get one or more professional degrees (law, medicine, dentistry, clinical psychology and the like) because the times

allowed your parents to more easily finance your degree with less risk and heartache, help your progeny whenever you are able to by rendering as much professional service as you can to them, if they choose not to follow you in your professional footsteps. In other words, degree sharing across generations.

13) Develop your "big picture" philosophy of life as early as you can. Tweak it, learn by trial and error, but by all means, live your philosophy!

14) Don't give up. Everyone you meet, at all levels of success and happiness, will tell you that giving up is the worst possible option. No exceptions!

15) The "existential" approach is wonderful from a personal, familial, professional and travel perspective. For purposes of amassing great financial wealth, not so good! I do suggest occasionally reading business magazines such as Forbes, Fortune and Barron's, especially if you can land a gift subscription.

16) Lighten up on sending your kids to "Ivy League" Schools. Take it from someone who attended his fair share of them. They're not quite as wonderful as they once were-and it's possible that your children may become a lot better adjusted and productive if they attend another fine liberal arts college or university which nurtures their particular individuality more appropriately.

17) Glen Beck, the oftentimes contentious and "more often right than wrong" talk show host, has stated that "Political correctness is killing this country." He further states that this anti-existentialist mode of looking at the world is clouding reality so much that one no longer can distinguish truth from legend. I agree with him.

18) Look at your life and that of those around you for the past ten (10) years. Note the changes, ups and downs, bumps along the way, births, deaths, illnesses, bankruptcies, accidents. Don't form any conclusions from such observations. Just contemplate them.

19) Be very wary of "Self-Improvement" books and tapes, especially those written by Hollywood celebrities. For example, a seemingly well intentioned work by Charles Grodin, movie actor and pundit, is laden with quotes and quips by scores of liberal Democrats and virtually no Republicans nor Libertarians, thereby putting into question the "existential honesty" of the writing. That book, like so many similar ones, appears to have a pre-ordained agenda, part of which is political, other parts philosophical.

20) Just be yourself. It always works as a solution to life's thorny problems. No self-help guru is better than just being yourself.

21) Hang loose. Especially in times of stress. And utilize "self-talk," an approach popularized by the late, great psychotherapist, Albert Ellis.

22) Become familiar with the works of the tortured Spanish Catholic existentialist, Miguel de Unamuno, even if you are not Catholic.

23) Join a health club/gym and make sure you focus on the sauna, steam room, Jacuzzi and swimming pool. Try a yoga class or two.

24) If your gall bladder is acting up, have it removed at once-no questions asked. You'll be glad you did.

25) Try to eliminate those self-serving holiday letters during the Christmas/Chanukah/Kwanzaa season. A simple card will suffice.

26) Take a deep breath. Engage in breathing and EFT (tapping) exercises as you deem appropriate. Contact me if you'd like further explanation on this one (PO Box 5265 Coralville, IA 52241)

27) Make and maintain contact with old high school or college friends and colleagues. Attend the reunions every so often.

28) Vacation in Las Vegas from time to time. It is both the antithesis and the essence of an existential experience.

29) The same can be said of Branson, Missouri, Wisconsin Dells and other tourist magnets.

30) Don't be impressed by the old farts who are still trying to impress you with their tired old tricks, pampered life styles and worn out symbols of success. It's a new world and it's changing every single minute.

31) If you believe in God, as I do, remember that he or she wants you to just be yourself.

32) Even if you don't believe in God, remember he or she wants you to just be yourself.

33) Always remember, you, the individual (and your family) are always more important than any other larger institution of which you are a constituent.

34) Are you getting the hang of these existential truisms yet? Try making up a few of your own.

35) Never give up the ship! The ship is your precious life.

36) Even if you think the future is bleak, don't let your children know it. Deal with your perception of reality by yourself, or with your trusted spouse or partner, if you are lucky enough to have a good one.

37) For the existential take on love, sex and marriage, I suggest you read my last novel, "The Optimistic Existentialist" or my next book, "Beyond Ideology." Even better, you should read Rollo May's classic, "Love and Will."

38) Late night coffee in a relatively empty, up-scale coffee shop is a good venue for "existential self-therapy."

39) I've drawn a blank on this one. But I recommend you listen to so-called "existential" rock and rollers of the 60's and 70's such as Neil Young, Bob Dylan, Jim Croce et al.

40) Use self-developed existential analysis as a tool for stress management.

41) Steer clear of "non-existentialist" self help books and tapes. They will always lead you down a path of deception.

42) I urge you to view some of the traditional films which depict an optimistic existential life style—"The Heartbreak Kid" with Charles Grodin, et al, "The Graduate", starring Dustin Hoffman, I Heart Huckabees with Dustin Hoffman again and L. Tomlin...and more.

43) I also urge you to check out two recently released existential films—even though they focus on the darker side of existential choices: "There Will Be Blood" and "No Country for Old Men."

44) Take personal charge of your health. Yes, existential philosophy works in this regard as well.

45) The earlier in the life span that you confront and resolve your "existential" dilemma(s), the better off you will be in the long run.

46) "All ill winds blow some good fate" from the novel "Silas Marner" by George Eliot.

47) "There is no pleasure so great as that which you believe you will not be enjoying for much longer." Tacitus, Roman historian.

48) Send post cards with short, sincere, thoughtful messages to people you meet along your path from interesting places you visit further along on your path.

49) Read my next book with additional and perhaps more revealing DOs and DON'Ts.

50) Keep on truckin'... And keep corporate America on the right track by persistently insisting on excellent customer service and by emphatically enforcing your contractual rights and those granted or reserved under the law.

51) At the time we were going to press, there occurred a series

of tragedies of unspeakable proportions all over America, even one in my own home town. Fathers of families brutally taking the lives of their wives and children and then apparently committing suicide in peculiar and equally brutal fashions. Without delving further into the particulars of the perpetrators and their victims, I feel obliged to offer some brief general rhetorical commentary with respect to these matters, since they so vitally impact upon human existence and upon existentialism.

The press, clergy, judicial system and numerous spin doctors and opinion makers seem to have given a total "pass" to the perpetrators of these horrific murders/suicides, assigning the causes thereof to be: "forgivable and temporary mental illness." Since the families of many of these presumed killers are deemed to be "prominent, wealthy, philanthropic and religious clans" with "great legacies" and inasmuch as the immediate families were often deemed to be "model" families prior to the occurrence of these incidents, the foregoing justifications seem to be acceptable to much of society.

But the fact remains that these explanations do not satisfactorily do justice to the perpetrators and the victims of these crimes and to society at large. Therefore, I pose the following rhetorical question and will leave my commentary at that:

Instead of propping up pre-packaged conceptualizations of family legacies and "model" families and explaining away unimaginable barbarism as a one time "mental illness" exception, can't we just re-examine said institutional models for so-called "success" to determine if there just might be something in those models that requires change, improvement or perhaps drastic overhaul.

I think we have a great opportunity here arising out of the ashes of these human disasters.

"All ill winds blow some good fate" from Silas Marner

Afterword—The Saga of Lena Hill

by Richard V. Campagna

I had originally intended to re-create the still ongoing history of a relationship/friendship I have maintained over the years with an adolescent girlfriend, hereinafter Lena Hill and her family. The Hills hail from Mansfield, Ohio or a similar town. I met Lena by chance at the spectacular Conquistador Hotel near Luquillo Beach, Puerto Rico during the winter of 1970 and was introduced to her family during an elegant dinner at the above-mentioned hotel soon thereafter.

Although we have had only 5 or 6 personal encounters over the forty years of our relationship (plus a few telephone calls, post cards and letters), our relationship has had a profound effect on my psyche, allowing me to more clearly understand the world in its "existential plenitude." I have learned so much about American life through our inter-actions, including but in no way limited to love, sex, gender, marriage, friendship, social class, business, politics, economics, treachery, substance abuse, materialism…you name it.

But alas, we have run out of time and space in this book, for this particular exercise. So I highly encourage you to do the following:

Rent and view the classic film, the original "Heartbreak Kid" starring Charles Grodin, Eddie Albert, Cybill Shepherd. View it alone or with your partner and try and imagine how my relationship with the Hill family parallels the trials and tribulations of the fictional character Lenny Cantrow and the Corcoran family in the film.

Feel free to contact me if you wish (Richard Campagna, PO Box 5265 Coralville, IA 52241) regarding the contents of this book and the relationship of the book and the above-mentioned film.

Finally, be on the lookout for my next book: "Beyond Ideology—The Genesis of An Existential Libertarian." I promise to include the full, instructive story alluded to above- no holds barred.

Peace, liberty, friendship until then.

Richard Campagna
Iowa City, Iowa
March, 2008

About the Author

Richard V. Campagna was born and raised in Brooklyn, N.Y. He graduated from Brown University in 1972 with a BA in political science and minors in Spanish and Portuguese. In 1975 he concurrently obtained a J.D. degree from St. John's University School of Law and an M.A. in Ibero-American Social Thought from New York University. Campagna went on to obtain a Masters degree in Counseling Psychology from Columbia University Teachers College and a "controversial" Ph.D. from the American College of Metaphysical Theology after pursuing additional graduate study at C.C.N.Y., Columbia University, the University of Iowa and the University of Chicago (Returning Scholar Program).

Campagna is fluent in Spanish, Portuguese, French, Italian and Papiamentu and has a working knowledge of Russian, Polish and Catalan. He is an accomplished legal, literary and medical interpreter and translator. He also serves as a corporate spokesperson, legal consultant, psychological counselor and college and career advisor. He teaches law, economics and ethics at various institutions of higher education. He is an avid traveller, having visited all 50 states and dependencies (on numerous occasions) and 199 foreign countries.

Campagna was the Libertarian Party's candidate for Lt. Governor of Iowa in 2002 (running mate of Clyde Cleveland) and ran for Vice President of the United States in 2004, also as a Libertarian (running mate Michael Badnarik).

Richard and his team of optimistic, pragmatic, spiritual, existentialist merrymakers have done it again. The author(s) set forth herein a low-key, workable philosophy of life (replete with DOs and DON'Ts) drawing from traditional existential philosophy, pop psychology from the 60's and 70's and novel practical approaches as well as personal, professional and political counsel, developed for the new millennium. A "minimalist" style of editing allows the "original flavor" of each contribution to shine through.

See 1stWorld Books at:

www.1stWorldPublishing.com

See our classic collection at:

www.1stWorldLibrary.org